Building Strong Foundations:

Personality Development For Students

Unlocking Personal Growth and Success Through Comprehensive Personality Development for Students

Dr. Ravindran.K.A.
HR Management Professional, Transformation Coach & Author

GUIDED SELF PUBLISHING (I) LLP

ISBN NO. 978-93-94808-52-2

MRP Rs.349/-   9.99$

Published by Guided Self Publishing (I) LLP, Sohna Haryana

Print & Distributed by Advika Book Mart

First edition Dec 10, 2024

Table of Contents

"Life isn't about finding yourself.
Life is about creating yourself"

George Bernard Shaw

Foreword

It is with great honour and enthusiasm that I present to you Building Strong Foundations: Personality Development for Students by Dr. Ravindran K.A. In a world that is constantly evolving, the need for comprehensive personal growth has never been more pressing, especially for students who are at a pivotal stage in their lives. Dr. Ravindran's work stands as a beacon of guidance for young minds seeking to understand not just the mechanics of academic success, but the deeper aspects of personal development that lead to lasting fulfillment and achievement.

Dr. Ravindran, an accomplished HR Management professional, Transformation Coach, and seasoned author, brings a wealth of experience to this book. His profound expertise in personal growth and organizational transformation is evident in every chapter, where he combines real-world insights with practical advice. With a deep passion for empowering others, he has crafted a guide that is both comprehensive and accessible, aimed at equipping students with the tools they need to succeed in all areas of life.

The subtitle, Unlocking Personal Growth and Success Through Comprehensive Personality Development for Students, encapsulates the essence of this book. Dr. Ravindran presents personality development as a holistic and lifelong journey. Far from being a mere collection of theoretical concepts, this book offers students a transformative roadmap—one that will not only enhance their academic capabilities but also shape their character, emotional intelligence, resilience, and relationships.

Through the sixteen chapters of this book, Dr. Ravindran explores a wide spectrum of critical topics—self-awareness, goal setting, effective communication, emotional intelligence, empathy, stress management, and more. Each chapter is thoughtfully designed to build upon the last, with practical exercises and real-life examples that make the process of self improvement both engaging and actionable. It is not just a book to read, but one to interact with and apply in everyday life.

What sets this book apart is its focus on a holistic approach to personality development. Dr. Ravindran recognizes that personal growth is not confined to academic performance or intellectual achievement alone. He emphasizes the importance of emotional and social intelligence, resilience in the face of adversity, and the development of a strong personal brand. These are qualities that are essential not only for academic success but for thriving in life's many challenges. In addressing topics such as embracing diversity, cultivating empathy, and building resilience, Dr. Ravindran provides students with the necessary skills to navigate the complexities of a rapidly changing world.

This book is a powerful tool not just for students, but for educators, mentors, and parents as well. Its reach goes beyond the classroom, encouraging a community-wide commitment to supporting the growth and development of young individuals. Dr. Ravindran's inclusive approach, which involves actionable strategies for students, parents, and teachers alike, fosters a supportive environment for personal transformation and growth.

Building Strong Foundations is more than just a guide to academic success—it is a mentor, a roadmap, and a source of inspiration for those embarking on the journey of self-discovery. It challenges students to go beyond their comfort zones, to reflect on their strengths and weaknesses, and to actively build a foundation that will support their dreams and aspirations.

In closing, I would like to commend Dr. Ravindran for this remarkable contribution. Building Strong Foundations is not merely a book; it is a call to action, a blueprint for a future filled with potential and possibility. I am confident that readers will find it to be a valuable resource as they embark on their own journey of personal and academic growth.

May this book inspire countless students to build the foundations of a successful, meaningful, and fulfilling life.

Sugandha Goel

Executive Director
Institute of Professional Excellence and Management, Ghaziabad, UP, India

Advance Praise for the Book

"Building Strong Foundations: Personality Development for Students" *is an invaluable resource for students striving for success and parents seeking guidance to support their children's growth. The book focuses on enhancing essential skills and offers a practical roadmap to help students tackle challenges and build a robust foundation for both their academic and professional journeys. Through its step-by-step approach in its 17 chapters, it helps students set and achieve personal goals while equipping them with life skills that extend beyond the classroom. Chapters such as Communication Skills, Time Management, and Continuous Self-Improvement provide valuable insights that will support students throughout their life journey. Teachers will undoubtedly recommend this book as a trusted guide, and students will cherish it as a cornerstone for their development.*

Dr. Ravindran K.A. brings a wealth of experience from the field of Human Resources (HR), having made significant contributions across various organizations. With a proven track record of fostering employee growth and development, he has chosen to share his expertise through a series of acclaimed HR books.

In ***"Building Strong Foundations: Personality Development for Students",*** *his fifth book, Dr. Ravindran shifts focus to the younger generation, offering insights that will help students grow into capable and accomplished professionals. His thoughtful guidance in this book is sure to inspire and empower its readers.*

My heartfelt congratulations to Dr. Ravindran K.A. on this remarkable achievement. I am confident that this book will be as impactful as his previous works and eagerly anticipate his next contribution. Wishing him continued success!

Punit Puri

HR Leader by passion, Mumbai, India

Social media plays a huge role in shaping how we see the world today, but it often gives a distorted sense of reality. Many young people are caught up in their own fantasy worlds, driven by platforms like Instagram Reels and YouTube Shorts. This overexposure affects their ability to focus and concentrate and as they grow into their teenage years, they often lack the life skills needed to handle situations with confidence and tact.

It's more important than ever to help students understand life's realities and guide them toward building a sense of purpose and positivity. Personality development is not something that happens overnight—it's a gradual, ongoing process. One simple but powerful step in this journey is reading.

That's why I'm so excited about the book "Building Strong Foundations: Personality Development for Students" by Dr. Ravindran. It's a fantastic resource for young minds, filled with practical advice to help them develop their personality, broaden their perspective, and face life with confidence.

I'm proud to recommend this book to students, parents, and teachers alike. I truly believe it will inspire young students to grow, improve, and transform themselves for the better. May it become a guiding light for all those who read it.

Abhirami K A

Assistant Professor

St. Aloysius College Thrissur, Kerala, India.

***"Building Strong Foundations: Personality Development for Students"** is a must-read book for every student who wants to be successful and achieve something with their life and also for every parent who wants their children to achieve success. It enhances the basic skills of the children and works as a guide that will help them face challenges and overcome them building a strong base for their student and professional life. It's a step-by-step guide to setting their personal goals and how to achieve them. The book equips children with critical life skills that will be utilized not only through their student life but also their personal lives. I am sure this book will become a treasured possession of students and will be highly recommended by teachers.*

*Author Dr. Ravindran KA has a vast experience in the Human Resources (HR) field. He has proven his mettle in different organizations that he has been part of. With a proven track record of planning employees' growth trajectories in a balanced way, he decided to share his vast experience with a wider audience. With this noble intention, he has published four books on HR Managing which are a must-read for every Management professional. His fifth book **"Building Strong Foundations: Personality Development for Students"** is for students and will definitely guide them to be better students and become accomplished professionals.*

My best wishes to Author Ravindran KA on his latest book. I am sure like all his earlier books, this book also will be highly useful to the intended beneficiaries. I wish him all success and eagerly await his next publication.

Sudhir Srivastava

Enterpreneur, Delhi, India

As a parent, watching my two girl children grow and evolve into the persons they are meant to be, has been one of the most rewarding experiences of my life. Along this journey, I have come to realize that personality development plays a pivotal role in shaping a child's future. The traits, values, and habits instilled early on, can make all the difference in how they approach challenges, build relationships, and navigate the world around them.

It is with great enthusiasm that I introduce this wonderful book on personality development. As a parent, I can wholeheartedly say that the insights shared within these pages are both valuable and timely. The wisdom, practical advice, and actionable strategies offered by the author Dr. Ravindran K A, who happens to be one of my college mates, provide an invaluable resource for anyone seeking to foster confidence, emotional intelligence, resilience, and self-awareness – qualities that are essential in today's fast-paced and often overwhelming world.

The author's approach to personality development is not only insightful but also deeply empathetic. As he rightly puts it in the book, the ability to understand oneself, build on one's strengths, and address areas for growth is a lifelong process, and this book serves as a guiding light on that path. I believe that every parent, teacher, and mentor would benefit from reading it, as it will not only enhance their own lives but also equip them to nurture the next generation with the tools needed to thrive.

I am grateful to the author for his dedication to helping young minds discover their true potential and for making this book a treasure trove of inspiration and encouragement.

With deep appreciation,

Suresh K,
An Employee of Amrita University, Coimbatore, Tamil Nadu, India

"Building Strong Foundations for Personal Development for Students" *by Dr. Ravindran K. A is an insightful resource for students aiming to cultivate their personal growth. Dr. Ravindran emphasizes the necessity of a solid foundation,* *which includes self-awareness, discipline, and resilience. His approach encourages students to focus on internal growth rather than external achievements, fostering a deeper understanding of their identity.*

The book is filled with practical exercises that promote self-reflection and goal-setting, making it accessible and engaging. Dr. Ravindran's motivational writing style inspires readers to embrace challenges as opportunities for growth. By integrating real-life examples, he illustrates how foundational skills can lead to lasting success.

Overall, this book serves as an essential guide for students, equipping them with the tools needed for lifelong personal development. Dr. Ravindran's expertise shines through, making this a valuable addition to any student's library as they navigate their personal and academic journeys.

Prof Dr Yogesh Kumar Gupta
IPEM Law Academy, Ghaziabad, UP, India

---

*It is my absolute pleasure to recommend the new book of dr. Ravindran ka's "**building strong foundations: personality development for students"***

I have known dr. Ravindran (ravi to me) since the last 22+ years now. He is a seasoned hr professional with around 3 decades of work experience in senior leadership roles, in various industries. He already has four books to his credit and several lectures delivered from impressive platforms.

*His current book, "**building strong foundations"** speaks about ' personality development for students" in his usual very simple way, complex issues are explained in a remarkable way and this moulds ones personality to brace up for difficult situations. This later will act as a guidepost in the journey ahead and make it easier to take the right decision, when called for.*

Various faces of self awareness are brought to light and the methods of further development are talked about in a clear, complete and concrete manner.

Several other important and vital aspects, like, effective communication, goal setting, and emotional intelligence have all been discussed and explained in this book. All these will later act as very strong and reliable support bridges for freshers (students), choosing to take on human resource management (hrm) as a career.

The journey of personality development will continue to be a lifelong affair. And accordingly, this book will prove valuable for all, especially young students, set to start their travel. They can keep this book as a personal guide and keep referring to the valuable tips given in this book.

The field of hrm is rapidly changing. Staying updated therefore is of prime importance for professionals and freshers alike, to be able to understand and handle various situations in a better way.

I enjoyed every chapter of this book and would like to say that it is a valuable collection of essential topics, highly readable and an absolute must for students.

*Wishing this new book, "**building strong foundations: personality development for students**" all success. May this also become a best seller.*

Blessings &

All good wishes

B. G. Menon

SENIOR MANAGER & DEPARTMENT HEAD

Shotam Consultants Pvt. Ltd.

---

*Dr. Ravindran K. A.'s work **on "Building a Strong Foundation for Personal Development for Students"** provides invaluable insights into the importance of developing self-awareness, emotional intelligence, and personal resilience in students. Through his research and practical guidance, Dr. Ravindran emphasizes the need for a holistic approach to education—one that goes beyond academics to focus on fostering personal growth. He highlights how essential it is for students to learn not only hard skills but also soft skills such as communication, problem-solving, and self-discipline. His methods encourage students to take charge of their learning journey, empowering them to overcome challenges and build a strong sense of purpose. The strategies outlined in his work serve as a blueprint for both educators and students, inspiring a culture of continuous growth and self-improvement. Dr. Ravindran's commitment to shaping well-rounded, confident individuals makes his approach essential for the development of future leaders.*

Prof Dr Geeti Sharma
Director IPEM Group of Institution, Ghaziabad, UP, India

Today's children are born in the digital age and are highly tech-savvy. Children are naturally curious and their inquiring minds drive their "Learning and Exploration. Another speciality of today's children is learning to navigate and express their emotions which can sometimes be overwhelming for them. However, they are social beings who thrive in interaction and collaboration with their peers and adults.

Nowadays parents play a vital role in providing emotional support, nurturing and guidance to their children. Effective communication and active listening between parents and children foster trust, understanding and strong bonds. A peculiarity of today's parents they need to establish clear boundaries and discipline to help children develop self-regulation skills and responsibility. Spending quality time and engaging in shared activities with parents helps children feel loved, valued and connected.

Children's relationships with their teachers are completely changed when compared to earlier generations. They often look up to their teachers with respect and admiration, seeking only guidance and approval. Building trust and maintaining open communication between teachers and students helps to create a supportive and inclusive learning environment. Teachers play a crucial role in providing positive reinforcement and developing confidence and self-esteem. Teachers serve as role models and mentors, inspiring children to learn grow and develop important life skills. In all these ways we can help children develop into confident, capable and compassionate individuals.

*These above factors have been amazingly presented by Author Dr. Ravindran.K.A, in his book titled **"Building Strong Foundations: Personality Development For Students".** I am sure this book will be a great guide to the students to improve and develop their personality and I wish a great success to this book and become a bestseller book.*

Femina Roy

Teacher of Government Higher Secondary School, Machad, Kerala, India.

---

*As a student, this book titled **"Building Strong Foundations: Personality Development For Students"** has been nothing short of transformative for me. This book is more than just a guide, it is a roadmap to discovering the best version of yourself. The emphasis on resilience, self-awareness and effective communication resonated deeply with me as these are not just for personal development but also a cornerstone of having a successful legal career. The one thing that most stuck with me is creating a vision board and setting specific goals as this has given me a structured approach to envisioning and working towards my career and in my academics. I highly recommend this book to students in all fields, but especially to those in law, where the interplay of intellect, empathy and resilience is critical. Thank you for inspiring students to dream big, stay focused and build a future.*

Ananya

5th Year of BBA, LLB Student, IP University, Delhi, India

The book ***"Building Strong Foundation: Personality Development for Students"*** *is a great way to introduce students, way different from a world where scepticism and validation from the outside world are way more celebrated, to a world of self-introspection where a student can reflect on his/her self and develop strong and healthy self-esteem. Carefully encrafted by Dr. Ravindran, the book in itself is a true guide for emerging minds and nascent thinkers coming from different walks of life to transform themselves into a confident, decisive and positive individual. In the due course of the book, it scrupulously answers the queries of curious, young minds by reflecting on various aspects necessary for holistic growth, for students which many times goes unanswered in real life. Highly recommendable and a fabulous self-help book for students where ideas are articulated in simple language and are true to their words.*

Wishing the book "Building Strong Foundation: Personality Development for Students" all the success and may it light up the lives of students and for all.

Greeshma Gopi
TGT English, Ryan International School, Mayur Vihar, Delhi, India

I am extremely happy to share that, I have read your book titled ***"Building Strong Foundations: Personality Development For Students".*** *Some key takeaways are:-*

- *Personality Development is a continuous journey, impacting all areas of life. The foundations built now will support students in achieving future success and personal fulfilment.*
- *The book encourages the students to create projects about their future dreams.*
- *Helps outside classroom development of a student.*

At last, I would like to share that the book is very helpful and amazing and wish a great success for this book.

Angad Chowdhary

Assistant Professor

IPEM LAW ACADEMY, Ghaziabad, UP, India

"This book is a transformative guide for any student seeking to unlock their potential and build a brighter future. The blend of practical exercises and relatable lessons makes it incredibly engaging, while the expert insights are invaluable for personal growth. Whether you're struggling with confidence or aiming to cultivate

resilience, this book has something for everyone. A must-read for students, parents, and educators alike!"

Surya

Student of BA, LLB 5th Semester, IPEM Law Academy, Ghaziabad, UP, India

---

"Dr. Ravindran has crafted a masterpiece that speaks directly to students' needs in today's fast-paced world. ***"Building Strong Foundations: Personality Development For Students"*** *doesn't just teach life skills; it inspires action and change. The strategies for emotional intelligence and goal setting are clear, actionable, and empowering. I highly recommend this book to anyone committed to achieving personal success and fulfillment."*

Dr Purnima Chaudhary,

Assistant Professor, IPEM Law Academy, Ghaziabad, UP, India

"This book titled ***"Building Strong Foundations: Personality Development For Students"*** *has completely changed the way I look at myself and my goals. The exercises are easy to follow, and the lessons on confidence and resilience have already helped me tackle challenges in school and life. I feel more motivated and focused than ever before. Every student who wants to grow and succeed should read this!"*

Himanshu

Student of BA, LLB 5th Semester, IPEM Law Academy, Ghaziabad, UP, India

---

Chapter 1
Understanding Personality Development

The Importance of Personality Development in Students

In today's competitive world, academic excellence alone is not enough to ensure success. Students also need to develop their personalities to stand out from the crowd and achieve their goals. Personality development plays a vital role in shaping the overall growth and success of students. This chapter aims to shed light on the importance of personality development for students, providing valuable insights for students, parents, teachers and trainers.

Personality development encompasses a wide range of skills and attributes, including communication, self-confidence, leadership, interpersonal skills and emotional intelligence. These qualities are not only critical for personal growth but also for professional success. Students with well-developed personalities are more likely to excel in interviews, presentations and collaborations, making them highly sought after by employers.

Developing a strong and vibrant personality is not a one-time process but rather a life-long journey. Parents, teachers and trainers play a vital role in guiding students through this journey. They can provide valuable guidance, support and mentorship to help students unlock their true potential. By encouraging students to participate in extracurricular activities, such as debates, sports and community service, they can help students develop crucial life skills and enhance their personalities.

Furthermore, personality development is not limited to classroom learning alone. It involves experiential learning, which allows students to explore and discover their strengths and weaknesses. By stepping out of their comfort zones, students can develop resilience, adaptability and problem-solving skills, which are essential for personal and professional growth.

Personality development also plays a crucial role in building healthy relationships and fostering empathy and understanding among students. By learning to communicate effectively, students can express their thoughts and ideas confidently, leading to better interpersonal relationships. The ability to empathize with others helps students develop a sense of compassion and tolerance, making them responsible and accomplished individuals.

In conclusion, personality development is of utmost importance for students in today's competitive world. It not only enhances their personal growth but also equips them with essential skills for success. Parents, teachers and trainers should actively support and guide students on their journey of personality development. By nurturing their strengths, encouraging participation in extracurricular activities and promoting experiential learning, we can help shape a generation of confident, empathetic and successful individuals.

Factors Influencing Personality Development in Students

Introduction:

In the journey of life, personality development plays a crucial role in shaping an individual's character, behaviour and overall success. As students embark on their educational path, it is essential to understand the various factors that influence their personality development. This chapter will delve into these influential factors, providing insights for students, parents, teachers and trainers who are dedicated to fostering optimal personality growth.

1. Genetic Factors:

Students inherit certain traits and characteristics from their parents, which serve as a foundation for their personality development. Genetic factors can influence aspects such as temperament, intelligence and tendencies towards certain behaviours, which should be acknowledged and nurtured accordingly.

2. Family Environment:

The family environment is a significant factor in shaping a student's personality. The dynamics, values and interactions within the family play a crucial role in the development of a student's self-esteem, confidence and social skills. Positive reinforcement, open communication and supportive relationships within the family can contribute to healthy personality development.

3. Peer Influence:

As students grow, their peers become an influential force in their lives. Peer pressure and the desire for acceptance can impact various aspects of personality development, including behaviour, decision-making and self-image. Encouraging positive peer relationships and teaching students to make independent choices can help them navigate peer influence effectively.

4. Educational Environment:

The educational environment, including school and classroom settings, contributes significantly to personality development. The teaching methods, curriculum and extracurricular activities in schools can shape students' self-confidence, leadership skills and overall personality traits. A supportive and inclusive educational environment can foster well-rounded personality development.

5. Cultural and Societal Influences:

Culture and society play a crucial role in shaping students' beliefs, values and behaviour patterns. Cultural traditions, societal norms and exposure to diverse perspectives impact the development of students' personalities. Encouraging cultural awareness and embracing diversity can help students develop a more inclusive and adaptable personality.

Conclusion:

Understanding the factors that influence personality development in students is vital for students, parents, teachers and trainers. By recognizing and nurturing these factors, individuals can create an environment conducive to optimal personality growth. Students can develop a strong sense of self, self-confidence and adaptability, enabling them to thrive academically and socially. Parents, teachers and trainers can play a pivotal role in supporting and guiding students throughout this journey, helping them build strong foundations for personality development.

The Role of Parents, Teachers and Trainers in Personality Development

In the journey of personality development, the role of parents, teachers and trainers is paramount. These individuals serve as the pillars of support and guidance, helping students build a strong foundation for their personal growth. By understanding the significance of their contribution, students, parents, teachers and trainers can work together harmoniously to foster a positive and nurturing environment for personality development.

Parents play a crucial role in shaping their child's personality. They are the first teachers, instilling values, morals and beliefs that lay the groundwork for personal development. Parents can create a loving and supportive atmosphere, providing encouragement and offering constructive criticism when needed. By setting clear expectations and boundaries, parents empower their children to develop discipline, responsibility and resilience. Consistent communication between parents and students is also vital, as it allows for the exchange of ideas and concerns, fostering a sense of belonging and emotional well-being.

Teachers, on the other hand, play a significant role in personality development within the school setting. They act as mentors and role models, imparting knowledge and skills that excel in the academic realm. Teachers have the power to inspire and ignite curiosity, helping students develop a thirst for learning and personal growth. Through effective teaching methods and individualized attention, teachers can identify and nurture the unique talents and strengths of each student. By fostering a classroom environment that promotes creativity, critical thinking and collaboration, teachers can help students develop self-confidence and a positive self-image.

Trainers, who often specialize in specific areas of personality development, offer valuable expertise and guidance to students. Whether it is in sports, arts or other extracurricular activities, trainers provide students with opportunities to explore their interests and develop their talents. Trainers offer specialized training, coaching and mentorship, helping students refine their skills and boost their self-esteem. Through their expertise, trainers can instill discipline, determination and a growth mindset in students, preparing them for success not only in their chosen field but also in life.

In conclusion, the role of parents, teachers and trainers in personality development is vital. By working together, they create a holistic and nurturing environment that supports students' personal growth. Students, parents, teachers and trainers must recognize the significance of their roles and strive to foster a positive and empowering atmosphere for personality development. Through collaboration and effective communication, they can build strong foundations for students' journey toward self-discovery and personal excellence.

Key Takeaways:

- Personality development is a life-long journey that starts with self-discovery.
- It involves understanding one's strengths, values and motivations, setting the stage for self-improvement.

Call to Action Exercises:

For Students:

1. **Self-Discovery Journal**: Write down three strengths and areas of improvement you observe in yourself.

   Strengths:

   ____

   ____

   ____

   Areas of improvement:

   ____

   ____

   ____

2. **Role Models**: Choose three role models and note traits you admire in them.

____

____

____

3. **Future Visualization**: How you Visualise yourself for the next five years from now and describe that vision.

____

____

____

____

____

____

____

____

____

____

For Parents:

1. **Observation Notebook**: Spend a week observing your child's strengths, then positively discuss them together.
2. **Encouragement Practice**: Identify one trait you value in your child and acknowledge it openly.
3. **Joint Activity**: Do an activity your child loves, helping them see how their personality shines.

For Teachers/Trainers:

1. **Strength Spotting**: Recognize and reinforce individual strengths during class activities.
2. **Open Discussion**: Start a class talk on personality traits and qualities students admire in others.
3. **Reflection Assignment**: Assign a brief reflection on three personal traits and their impact on school life.

Chapter 2 : Self-Awareness and Self-Reflection

Understanding Self-Awareness

Self-awareness is a crucial aspect of personality development for students. It encompasses the ability to recognize and understand one's emotions, thoughts and behaviours. By cultivating self-awareness, students can gain a deeper understanding of themselves, their strengths, weaknesses and values. This chapter highlights the significance of self-awareness and provides valuable insights for students, parents, teachers and trainers.

For students, self-awareness serves as a compass, guiding them towards personal growth and success. By becoming more aware of their own emotions and reactions, they can effectively manage their feelings and make informed decisions. Self-awareness encourages students to take responsibility for their actions and fosters a sense of accountability. It also enables them to recognize their strengths and weaknesses, allowing them to capitalize on their strengths and work on improving areas that need development.

Parents play a vital role in supporting their children's journey towards self-awareness. By fostering an open and non-judgmental environment, parents can encourage their children to explore their emotions and thoughts. They can help students identify their passions, interests and values, enabling them to make choices that align with their true selves. Parents can also guide their children in setting realistic goals and provide constructive feedback to help them grow personally and academically.

Teachers and trainers have a unique opportunity to promote self-awareness in the classroom. By incorporating reflective exercises, such as journaling or group discussions, educators can encourage students to delve deeper into their thoughts and emotions. This can enhance their critical thinking skills and empathy towards others. Teachers can also provide constructive feedback and encourage self-reflection, enabling students to identify areas for improvement and develop a growth mindset.

Furthermore, for trainers working in the niche of personality development for students, understanding and fostering self-awareness is essential. By designing workshops or training sessions that promote self-reflection and introspection, trainers can help students uncover their true potential. They can facilitate activities that encourage students to explore their values, beliefs and goals, enabling them to develop a strong sense of identity.

In conclusion, self-awareness is a fundamental aspect of personality development for students. By understanding and cultivating self-awareness, students can navigate their journey towards personal growth and success. Parents, teachers and trainers all play crucial roles in supporting and guiding students in their quest for self-awareness. By providing the necessary tools and creating a safe space, they can empower students to develop a deep understanding of themselves and make choices that align with their true selves.

Techniques for Developing Self-Awareness

Self-awareness is a fundamental aspect of personality development for students. It involves understanding one's own thoughts, emotions, strengths and weaknesses. By developing self-awareness, students can gain a deeper understanding of themselves, which will ultimately lead to personal growth and success. In this chapter, we will explore various techniques that can help students cultivate self-awareness.

1. Reflection: Encourage students to set aside time for self-reflection. This can be done through journaling, meditation or simply taking a moment to think about their day. Reflection allows students to process their thoughts and emotions, helping them gain insight into their own behaviour and decisions.

2. Feedback: Encourage students to seek feedback from trusted individuals, such as parents, teachers or mentors. Constructive feedback provides students with an external perspective on their strengths and areas for improvement. By listening to and considering feedback, students can gain a better understanding of how they are perceived by others.

3. Strengths and Weaknesses Assessment: Help students identify their strengths and weaknesses. This can be

done through self-assessment tools, such as personality tests or skills assessments. Understanding their strengths will boost their confidence while acknowledging weaknesses will help them focus on areas that need improvement.

4. Mindfulness: Teach students the practice of mindfulness, which involves being fully present in the moment. Mindfulness allows students to observe their thoughts and emotions without judgment. This practice helps students develop a greater sense of self-awareness and control over their actions.

5. Self-Expression: Encourage students to express themselves creatively through art, writing or any other medium they enjoy. Self-expression enables students to explore their inner thoughts and emotions, leading to a deeper understanding of themselves.

6. Goal Setting: Assist students in setting realistic and achievable goals. By setting clear goals, students can monitor their progress and evaluate their strengths and weaknesses along the way. This process promotes self-awareness as students become more tuned to their abilities and areas that require improvement.

7. Seeking Challenges: Encourage students to step out of their comfort zones and embrace new challenges. Facing unfamiliar situations allows students to discover their strengths and weaknesses, fostering self-awareness and personal growth.

By implementing these techniques, students can develop a strong foundation of self-awareness. This newfound self-awareness will not only contribute to their personal growth but also empower them to make informed decisions, build healthy relationships and excel academically and professionally. Parents, teachers and trainers play a crucial role in guiding and supporting students in their journey towards self-discovery and self-awareness.

The Power of Self-Reflection

In the journey of personality development for students, one of the most powerful tools at our disposal is self-reflection. It is the practice of looking inward, examining our thoughts, emotions and actions, to gain a deeper understanding of ourselves. By engaging in self-reflection, students can develop a strong foundation for personal growth, self-awareness and success in various aspects of life.

Self-reflection allows students to pause and evaluate their experiences, accomplishments and challenges. It provides an opportunity to learn from past mistakes and make better decisions in the future. By taking the time to reflect on their actions and behaviours, students can identify patterns and make necessary changes to improve themselves.

Through self-reflection, students can gain a clearer understanding of their strengths and weaknesses. By recognizing their strengths, they can build upon them and use them to their advantage. Similarly, by acknowledging their weaknesses, they can work towards overcoming them and turning them into strengths. This process helps students develop a positive self-image and boosts their self-confidence.

Self-reflection also enables students to develop empathy and understanding towards others. By reflecting on their own experiences and emotions, students can relate to the experiences of their peers and develop a sense of compassion. This enhances their interpersonal skills and allows them to build strong relationships with their classmates, teachers and family members.

Furthermore, self-reflection encourages students to set and achieve goals. By reflecting on their progress, students can assess whether they are on the right track towards their objectives. It helps them identify the steps they need to take to reach their goals and motivates them to stay focused and determined.

For parents, teachers and trainers, encouraging students to engage in self-reflection is vital. By providing them with the necessary guidance and creating a supportive environment, educators can help students develop self-awareness and cultivate a habit of self-reflection. This, in turn, will contribute to their overall personal growth and development.

In conclusion, the power of self-reflection cannot be underestimated in the realm of personality development for students. It allows students to gain insights into their thoughts, emotions and behaviours, leading to self-awareness, personal growth and success. By incorporating self-reflection into their daily lives, students can lay a strong foundation for their future endeavours and unlock their full potential.

Key Takeaways:

- Self-awareness helps individuals understand who they are and why they behave a certain way.
- Regular self-reflection allows for growth by examining strengths, weaknesses and motivations.

Call to Action Exercises:

For Students:

1. **Daily Reflection**: Spend five minutes daily reflecting on how you felt and behaved.
2. **Weekly Journaling**: Note one achievement and one lesson learned every week.
3. **Mindfulness Exercise**: Practice a short breathing exercise to build awareness of your thoughts.

For Parents:

1. **Model Self-Reflection**: Share a story where self-reflection helped you grow.
2. **Encourage Honest Conversations**: Create an environment where your child feels comfortable sharing their feelings.

3. **Reflect Together**: Set aside time to reflect with your child on one positive experience and what they learned.

For Teachers/Trainers:

1. **Class Reflection Time**: Set aside five minutes after an activity for students to reflect.
2. **Individual Feedback**: Encourage students to think about what went well and where they can improve.
3. **Self-Awareness Worksheet**: Provide a worksheet on self-reflection to help students to analyze their strengths.

Chapter 3: Setting Goals and Creating a Vision

The Significance of Goal-Setting for Students

In today's fast-paced and highly competitive world, goal-setting has become an essential skill for students to thrive academically, personally and professionally.

Building Strong Foundations: Personality Development for Students emphasizes the importance of goal-setting as a vital tool for success. This chapter aims to shed light on the significance of goal-setting for students and how it enhances their overall personality development.

Goal-setting provides students with a clear direction and purpose. By setting specific, measurable, attainable, relevant and time-bound (SMART) goals, students gain focus and motivation in their studies and extracurricular activities. Goals act as a roadmap, guiding students towards their desired achievements. They provide a sense of purpose and help students prioritize tasks, manage their time effectively and stay on track.

Setting goals also helps students develop a growth mindset. When students set goals, they learn to embrace challenges and view failures as opportunities for growth. It fosters resilience and perseverance, enabling students to bounce back from setbacks and continue their journey towards success. By setting small, achievable goals, students build self-confidence and develop a positive attitude towards learning and personal growth.

Goal-setting instills a sense of responsibility and accountability in students. When they set goals, they take ownership of their learning process and become proactive in seeking opportunities for improvement. They become more self-disciplined, as they understand the importance of consistent effort and dedication in achieving their goals. This sense of responsibility extends beyond academics, as students learn to set goals in various aspects of their lives, such as health, relationships and personal development.

Furthermore, goal-setting enhances students' decision-making skills. When students have a clear vision of their goals, they can make informed choices aligned with their aspirations. It helps them avoid distractions and make choices that contribute to their long-term success. By setting goals, students become more focused, disciplined and determined, which ultimately leads to improved academic performance and personal growth.

For parents, teachers and trainers, understanding the significance of goal-setting empowers them to support students in their journey of personality development. By assisting students in setting realistic and achievable goals, they can guide them towards success and foster a growth mindset. Encouraging students to reflect on their goals, track their progress and celebrate milestones creates a positive learning environment that promotes self-confidence and motivation.

In conclusion, goal-setting plays a key role in the personality development of students. It provides them with a sense of direction, fosters a growth mindset, instills responsibility and accountability, enhances decision-making skills and improves overall academic performance. Embracing goal-setting as an integral part of students' lives empowers them to become self-directed learners, motivated achievers and well-rounded individuals, ready to face the challenges of the world.

Strategies for Setting Realistic and Achievable Goals

Setting goals is an important aspect of personal and professional development. Whether you are a student, parent, teacher or trainer, understanding how to set realistic and achievable goals can help you build a strong foundation for personality development. In this chapter, we will explore effective strategies that can assist individuals in setting and reaching their goals.

1. Define your goals: The first step in goal setting is to clearly define what you want to achieve. Take some time to reflect on your aspirations and identify specific, measurable, attainable, relevant and time-bound (SMART) goals. Being specific and clear about your objectives will provide you with a sense of direction and purpose.

2. Break it down: Once you have identified your main goal, break it down into smaller and manageable tasks. This approach will make your goals less

overwhelming and more achievable. Create a timeline and prioritize these tasks to ensure steady progress towards your ultimate goal.

3. Stay motivated: Maintaining motivation is crucial when it comes to achieving your goals. Find ways to keep yourself inspired and focused. Celebrate small victories along the way and surround yourself with positive influences that support your journey towards success.

4. Seek feedback and support: Don't be afraid to seek feedback from mentors, teachers or trainers who can provide constructive criticism and guidance. Surround yourself with a supportive network that can help you stay accountable and motivated. Remember, asking for help is a sign of strength, not weakness.

5. Learn from setbacks: Setbacks are inevitable, but they should not deter you from your goals. Instead, view them as valuable learning opportunities. Analyze the reasons behind your setbacks and adapt your strategies accordingly. Embrace the growth mindset, which sees failures as stepping stones towards success.

6. Review and revise: Regularly review your progress and make necessary revisions to your goals. As you grow and change, your objectives may evolve as well. Be flexible and open to adjusting your path to

ensure it aligns with your current values and aspirations.

By implementing these strategies, you will be better equipped to set realistic and achievable goals. Remember, the journey towards personal growth and development is unique for each individual. Embrace your strengths, stay focused and believe in yourself. Building a strong foundation for personality development starts with setting meaningful goals and working towards them with determination and resilience.

Developing a Vision for Personal Growth

In the journey of life, personal growth is a vital aspect that allows individuals to reach their full potential. It encompasses various aspects such as self-awareness, self-improvement and the development of essential skills and qualities. To embark on this path of personal growth, it is essential to have a clear vision that acts as a guiding light, directing your efforts towards success. This chapter explores the significance of developing a vision for personal growth and provides practical insights for students, parents, teachers and trainers in the niche of personality development.

For students, having a vision for personal growth is crucial as it helps in setting goals, staying focused and making informed decisions about their future. By understanding their strengths, weaknesses and aspirations, students can develop a vision that aligns with their passion and purpose.

This vision acts as a roadmap, enabling them to make the right choices and seize opportunities that contribute to their personal and academic growth.

Parents play a vital role in supporting their child's personal growth journey. By assisting their children in identifying their interests, values and long-term goals, parents can help shape a vision that aligns with their child's unique talents and potential. They can also provide the necessary resources, encouragement and guidance to help their children stay motivated and overcome challenges along the way.

Teachers and trainers have a significant influence on students' personal growth. By fostering an environment that promotes self-discovery, critical thinking and goal-setting, educators can empower students to develop their vision for personal growth. They can facilitate discussions, provide mentorship and offer guidance on various aspects of personal development, such as time management, effective communication and resilience.

To develop a vision for personal growth, individuals need to reflect on their values, passions and long-term aspirations. They should envision the kind of person they want to become and the impact they wish to create in their personal and professional lives. It is essential to set both short-term and long-term goals that are specific, measurable, achievable, relevant and time-bound (SMART).

In conclusion, developing a vision for personal growth is a transformative process that empowers individuals to realize their true potential. Whether you are a student, parent, teacher or trainer in the niche of personality development, understanding the significance of a clear vision and its role in personal growth is crucial. By guiding students to develop their vision, we can equip them with the necessary tools and mindset to navigate through life, overcome obstacles and achieve their dreams.

Key Takeaways:

- Goal-setting provides direction and helps one visualize a successful journey.
- Creating a clear vision helps maintain focus on long-term growth and development.

Call to Action Exercises:

For Students:

1. **Personal Goals List**: Write down three short-term and three long-term goals.

Short-term Goals	
1	
2	
3	
Long-term Goals	
1	
2	
3	

2. **Vision Board**: Create a visual representation of your goals to stay motivated.

3. **Progress Tracker**: Make a plan to review and update your goals every month.

For Parents:

1. **Goal Support**: Talk with your child about their goals and how you can support them.
2. **Encourage Small Wins**: Celebrate small achievements on the path to bigger goals.
3. **Family Vision Board**: Create a family vision board together, each contributing personal goals.

For Teachers/Trainers:

1. **Class Goal Setting**: Discuss and set a class goal for the term.
2. **Achievement Recognition**: Recognize students when they make progress toward their goals.
3. **Future Planning Exercise**: Lead students in creating their own 5-year plan.

Chapter 4
Building Confidence and Self-Esteem

Understanding Confidence and Self-Esteem

Confidence and self-esteem are two essential elements of personality development for students. In today's competitive world, students must understand the importance of building a strong foundation in these areas. This chapter aims to explore the concept of confidence and self-esteem, how they interrelate and how they can be nurtured.

Confidence is the belief in oneself and one's abilities. It is the assurance that you can handle different situations and challenges that come your way. Self-esteem, on the other hand, is the value and respect one has for oneself. It is the overall perception of one's worth and the belief that one deserves happiness and success.

Confidence and self-esteem are closely connected. When you have confidence in your abilities, it enhances your self-esteem. Likewise, when you have a healthy level of self-esteem, it boosts your confidence. It is important to understand that confidence and self-esteem are not fixed traits; they can be developed and improved over time.

Students, parents, teachers and trainers all play a significant role in nurturing confidence and self-esteem. Parents and teachers need to provide a supportive and encouraging environment for students. They should recognize and celebrate their achievements, no matter how small and provide constructive feedback to help them grow. Trainers can also contribute by providing students with opportunities to develop their skills and talents through various activities.

To build confidence and self-esteem, students need to set realistic goals and work towards achieving them. It is essential to challenge oneself and step out of the comfort zone, as this is where personal growth occurs. Students should also surround themselves with positive and supportive individuals who believe in their abilities and provide guidance when needed.

Additionally, self-care and self-reflection are vital aspects of building confidence and self-esteem. Students should take care of their physical and mental well-being by engaging in activities they enjoy, practising mindfulness and seeking help when needed. They should also reflect on their strengths and accomplishments, as this fosters a positive self-image.

In conclusion, confidence and self-esteem are crucial elements for students' personality development. By understanding the significance of these traits and actively working towards building them, students can unlock their full potential. With the support and guidance of parents, teachers and trainers; students can develop a strong foundation of confidence and self-esteem, allowing them to navigate through challenges and embrace success in all aspects of life..

Techniques for Boosting Confidence

Introduction:

Confidence is a key attribute that plays a crucial role in the overall personality development of students. It empowers them to face challenges, overcome obstacles and achieve their goals. In this chapter, we will explore various techniques that can help students boost their confidence levels. These techniques are designed to be practical, effective and applicable to students of all ages and backgrounds. Whether you are a student, parent, teacher or trainer, incorporating these techniques into your daily routine will contribute to the holistic personality development of students.

1. Positive Self-Talk:

Encouraging students to engage in positive self-talk is an effective technique for boosting confidence. By replacing negative thoughts with positive affirmations, students can reframe their mindset and build a stronger belief in themselves. Encourage them to identify their strengths, acknowledge their accomplishments and focus on their potential rather than dwelling on their shortcomings.

2. Goal Setting and Achievement:

Setting achievable goals and working towards them is a powerful way to boost confidence. Encourage students to break down their larger goals into smaller, manageable tasks. As they accomplish each task, they will experience a sense of achievement, which in turn enhances their confidence levels. Teach them to celebrate these small victories and learn from any setbacks along the way.

3. Embracing Failure as a Learning Opportunity:

Failure is a natural part of life and students need to understand that setbacks do not define them. Encourage them to view failure as a learning opportunity rather than a reflection of their abilities. By shifting their perspective, students can develop resilience, learn from their mistakes and grow their confidence in their ability to overcome challenges.

4. Emphasizing Personal Growth:

Help students understand that confidence is not merely based on external validation but is rooted in their personal growth and progress. Encourage them to focus on self-improvement rather than comparing themselves to others. By setting their own benchmarks and working towards self-defined goals, students can enhance their confidence and develop a healthy sense of self-worth.

5. Encouraging Positive Peer Interactions:

A supportive peer network plays a significant role in boosting confidence. Encourage students to surround themselves with positive and uplifting individuals who inspire and motivate them. By fostering healthy relationships, students can build a strong support system that strengthens their confidence and helps them navigate challenges more effectively.

Conclusion:

Confidence is a vital attribute that students need to develop to succeed in various aspects of life. By incorporating these techniques into their lives, students can enhance their self-belief, overcome challenges and thrive academically and personally. As parents, teachers and trainers, it is crucial to provide guidance, support and encouragement to help students build strong foundations of confidence. By doing so, we empower them to reach their full potential and become well-rounded individuals equipped to face the world with confidence and resilience.

Overcoming Self-Doubt and Developing Self-Esteem

Introduction:

In today's fast-paced and competitive world, students must develop strong personalities that can withstand challenges and setbacks. One of the essential aspects of personality development is overcoming self-doubt and nurturing self-esteem. This chapter aims to provide valuable insights and practical strategies to help students overcome self-doubt and build a healthy sense of self-worth. Whether you are a student, parent, teacher or trainer, understanding and implementing these principles can significantly contribute to the overall personality development of students.

Understanding Self-Doubt:

Self-doubt is a common experience that can hinder personal growth and success. It often stems from fear of failure, comparison to others or negative past experiences. Students may doubt their abilities, intelligence or worthiness, leading to a lack of confidence and motivation. By acknowledging and understanding self-doubt, individuals can take the first step towards overcoming it.

Strategies for Overcoming Self-Doubt:

1. Identify and challenge negative self-talk: Students must recognize their inner critic and replace negative thoughts with positive affirmations. Encourage them to focus on their strengths and accomplishments, fostering a growth mindset.

2. Set achievable goals: Breaking larger goals into smaller, attainable ones helps combat self-doubt. Celebrating each milestone achieved along the way boosts confidence and motivation.

3. Surround yourself with positive influences: Encourage students to seek supportive relationships with friends, family, teachers and mentors who believe in their abilities. Positive reinforcement and encouragement can do wonders for self-esteem.

Developing Self-Esteem:

Self-esteem is the foundation of a strong personality. It is the belief in one's worth and capabilities. Developing self-esteem is crucial for students' overall well-being and success in various aspects of life.

Strategies for Developing Self-Esteem:

1. Practice self-care: Encourage students to prioritize their physical and mental health. Regular exercise, proper nutrition and sufficient sleep play a significant role in boosting self-esteem.

2. Embrace mistakes and failures: Students should understand that failure is a stepping stone to success. Encourage them to learn from mistakes and view setbacks as opportunities for growth and improvement.

3. Engage in activities that bring joy and fulfillment: Pursuing hobbies and interests outside of academics helps students build a sense of accomplishment and satisfaction, boosting self-esteem.

Conclusion:

Overcoming self-doubt and developing self-esteem are vital aspects of personality development for students. By implementing the strategies outlined in this chapter, students can break free from self-imposed limitations and unlock their full potential. Parents, teachers and trainers play a crucial role in supporting and guiding students through this journey. Together, let us create an environment that fosters self-belief, resilience and unwavering confidence in students, enabling them to build strong foundations for a successful future.

Key Takeaways:

- Confidence grows from self-acceptance and a positive self-image.
- Self-esteem can be improved through practice, patience and self-compassion.

Call to Action Exercises:

For Students:

1. **Daily Affirmations**: Write three positive affirmations and repeat them daily.

   i)

   ii)

   iii)

2. **Strengths List**: List five personal strengths and revisit them often.

   i)

   ii)

   iii)

   iv)

   v)

3. **Confidence Challenge**: Try something new every week to build confidence in your abilities.

For Parents:

1. **Celebrate Efforts**: Acknowledge your child's efforts, not just their results.
2. **Positive Feedback**: Use positive language to help your child feel valued and appreciated.
3. **Encourage Self-Praise**: Encourage your child to express pride in their accomplishments.

For Teachers/Trainers:

1. **Public Praise**: Give specific praise in class, highlighting students' achievements.
2. **Peer Recognition Activity**: Have students share positive qualities they see in each other.
3. **Confidence-Boosting Task**: Assign tasks that help students recognize their strengths.

Chapter 5: Effective Communication Skills

The Importance of Communication Skills in Personality Development

Communication skills are an essential aspect of personality development for students. The ability to effectively communicate not only helps in expressing thoughts and ideas but also plays a crucial role in building relationships, resolving conflicts and achieving success in various areas of life. In this chapter, we will explore the significance of communication skills and how they contribute to the overall personality development of students.

First and foremost, strong communication skills empower students to express themselves confidently and articulately. Whether it is participating in class discussions, giving presentations or engaging in debates, students who possess good communication skills are more likely to stand out and make a lasting impression. Effective communication also enhances critical thinking and problem-solving abilities, as it requires students to analyze information, evaluate different perspectives and present logical arguments.

Furthermore, communication skills are vital in building and maintaining relationships. Students who can communicate effectively are better equipped to establish connections with their peers, teachers and even their parents. This enables them to work collaboratively, seek help when needed and foster a positive learning environment. Good communication skills also enable students to empathize with others, understand different viewpoints and resolve conflicts amicably.

In the professional world, employers highly value individuals with strong communication skills. Whether it is writing clear and concise emails, delivering impactful presentations or working in teams, effective communication is a fundamental requirement in almost every job. By developing excellent communication skills early on, students are better prepared for future career opportunities and can effectively convey their thoughts, ideas and achievements to potential employers.

As parents, teachers and trainers, it is essential to recognize the significance of communication skills in personality development. Encouraging students to participate in extracurricular activities such as debates, drama or public speaking can greatly enhance their communication abilities. Additionally, incorporating communication-focused exercises and activities into the curriculum can provide students with ample opportunities to practice and improve their skills.

In conclusion, communication skills are paramount in personality development for students. They not only help in expressing thoughts and ideas effectively but also contribute to the building of relationships, conflict resolution and future career success. By emphasizing the importance of communication skills and providing ample opportunities for practice, we can empower students to become confident, articulate and successful individuals in all facets of life.

Verbal Communication Skills

Effective communication is an essential skill that plays a significant role in our personal and professional lives. In today's fast-paced world, being able to articulate thoughts and ideas clearly and confidently is crucial for success. This chapter on "Verbal Communication Skills" aims to provide students, parents, teachers and trainers with valuable insights into developing strong verbal communication abilities.

The chapter begins by emphasizing the importance of verbal communication skills in various aspects of life. Whether it's expressing oneself in class, participating in group discussions or delivering presentations, effective verbal communication can boost self-confidence, foster meaningful relationships and open doors to countless opportunities.

Next, the chapter delves into the essential elements of effective verbal communication. It explores the significance of clarity, tone, body language and active listening. Students will learn how to choose words wisely, maintain an engaging and confident tone and use appropriate body language to effectively convey their message. Moreover, they will understand the importance of attentive listening, which not only demonstrates respect but also enhances understanding and promotes effective communication.

Furthermore, the chapter provides practical tips and exercises to improve verbal communication skills. From practising public speaking to engaging in debates and discussions, students will learn how to overcome fear and develop confidence in expressing their ideas. The chapter also offers guidance on effective storytelling, using visual aids and adapting communication styles to different audiences.

To reinforce the importance of verbal communication skills, real-life examples and success stories will be shared throughout the chapter. These anecdotes will inspire and motivate students, parents, teachers and trainers to continuously work on honing their communication abilities.

Lastly, the chapter concludes by highlighting the benefits of developing strong verbal communication skills. Whether it's acing a job interview, building strong relationships or becoming an influential leader, effective verbal communication skills are essential for personal and professional growth.

In summary, this chapter on "Verbal Communication Skills" in the book "Building Strong Foundations: Personality Development for Students" aims to equip students, parents, teachers and trainers with the necessary tools to enhance their verbal communication abilities. By mastering effective communication skills, individuals can build strong foundations for success in all areas of life.

Valuable Insights into honing and enhancing these Verbal Communication Skills:

Developing strong verbal communication abilities is crucial for success in various aspects of life, including academic, professional and personal interactions. Here are valuable insights into honing and enhancing these skills:

1. Active Listening:

- Insight: Effective verbal communication begins with active listening. Understanding the importance of truly hearing what others are saying is foundational to meaningful conversations.

- Practice: Train yourself to focus on the speaker without formulating your response prematurely. Repeat key points to confirm understanding and ask clarifying questions to demonstrate engagement.

2. Clarity and Conciseness:

- Insight: Clear and concise communication minimizes the risk of misunderstandings. Being articulate and to the point enhances the impact of your message.

- Practice: Practice straightforwardly expressing ideas. Eliminate unnecessary details and ensure your message is easily comprehensible to diverse audiences.

3. Vocabulary and Language Choice:

- Insight: A rich and varied vocabulary enhances communication, but it's essential to choose words appropriate for your audience. Effective verbal communication involves tailoring your language to the context.

- Practice: Expand your vocabulary by reading diverse materials. Practice using different levels of language depending on whether you're communicating with peers, superiors or a general audience.

4. Non-Verbal Signs:

- Insight: Non-verbal cues, including body language, facial expressions and gestures, significantly contribute to the overall message. Understanding and utilizing these signs enhances the clarity of communication.

- Practice: Pay attention to your own non-verbal cues and those of others. Ensure that your body language aligns with your spoken words. Practice maintaining eye contact and using gestures purposefully.

5. Empathy and Emotional Intelligence:

- Insight: Verbal communication is not just about words; it's about connecting emotionally. Empathy allows you to understand and respond appropriately to others' emotions.

- Practice: Cultivate empathy by actively considering others' perspectives. Acknowledge emotions in both yourself and others and respond with sensitivity.

6. Adaptability and Flexibility:

- Insight: Effective communicators adapt their style to fit different situations and audiences. Flexibility in communication ensures your message resonates with diverse groups.

- Practice: Experiment with adjusting your communication style based on the context. Pay attention to how others respond and be willing to modify your approach as needed.

7. Confidence and Assertiveness:

- Insight: Confidence in your communication instills trust and credibility. Being assertive allows you to express your thoughts and needs with clarity and conviction.

- Practice: Work on developing a confident speaking voice. Practice assertive communication by expressing your thoughts in a straightforward yet respectful manner.

8. Effective Use of Technology:

- Insight: In today's digital age, verbal communication often extends to virtual platforms. Mastering the use of technology enhances your ability to convey messages through various channels.

- Practice: Familiarize yourself with video conferencing tools, voice messaging and other digital communication platforms. Practice effective communication in virtual environments.

9. Constructive Feedback:

- Insight: Giving and receiving feedback is an integral part of effective verbal communication. Constructive feedback promotes growth and improvement.

- Practice: Practice providing feedback positively and constructively. Learn to receive feedback graciously and use it as an opportunity for personal and professional development.

10. Public Speaking Skills:

- Insight: Public speaking is a valuable skill that extends beyond formal presentations. It involves conveying ideas confidently and engagingly in various settings.

- Practice: Join public speaking clubs, participate in group discussions and take on opportunities to speak in front of others. Practice structuring your thoughts for clarity and delivering them with conviction.

By incorporating these insights into your approach to verbal communication and consistently practising them, you can develop strong communication abilities that contribute to success in your academic, professional and personal endeavours.

What are the essential elements of effective verbal communication?

Effective verbal communication is crucial for conveying messages clearly and building meaningful connections. Several essential elements contribute to successful verbal communication:

1. Clarity:

- Definition: Clear communication ensures that the message is easily understood by the listener.

- Importance: Ambiguity and unclear expressions can lead to misunderstandings. A clear message minimizes the chances of misinterpretation.

2. Conciseness:

- Definition: Expressing ideas in a brief and to-the-point manner without unnecessary details.

- Importance: Concise communication respects the listener's time and maintains their attention. It prevents information overload and facilitates a better understanding of the key points.

3. Active Listening:

- Definition: Actively engaging with the speaker, showing attention and comprehension.

- Importance: Active listening fosters a two-way communication process, demonstrating respect and ensuring that the message is received accurately. It also encourages open dialogue.

4. Non-Verbal Cues:

- Definition: Facial expressions, body language, gestures and tone of voice that accompany spoken words.

- Importance: Non-verbal cues complement verbal communication, conveying emotions, emphasis and additional information. They enhance the overall message and help interpret the speaker's intentions.

5. Empathy:

- Definition: Understanding and sharing the feelings of the speaker.

- Importance: Empathetic communication creates a connection between individuals. It involves acknowledging emotions, demonstrating understanding and responding with sensitivity; fostering a positive communication environment.

6. Feedback:

- Definition: The response or reaction to a message, indicating how well it was understood.

- Importance: Constructive feedback allows the speaker to gauge the effectiveness of their communication. It helps in clarifying points, adjusting messages and improving future communication.

7. Adaptability:

- Definition: Adjusting communication style based on the audience, context or feedback received.

- Importance: Adaptable communication ensures that the message resonates with diverse audiences. It demonstrates flexibility and a willingness to tailor communication for optimal understanding.

8. Confidence:

- Definition: Speaking with assurance and self-assuredness.

- Importance: Confidence infuses trust and credibility. It helps the speaker convey their message with conviction, capturing the listener's attention and enhancing the overall impact.

9. Appropriate Tone:

- Definition: The emotional quality or pitch of the speaker's voice.

- Importance: The tone sets the emotional context of the message. An appropriate tone ensures that the listener accurately interprets the speaker's intended emotions, preventing misunderstandings.

10. Cultural Sensitivity:

- Definition: Awareness and respect for cultural differences in communication styles and norms.

- Importance: In a globalized world, understanding and respecting diverse cultural perspectives is crucial. Cultural sensitivity prevents unintentional misunderstandings and promotes effective cross-cultural communication.

11. Logical Structure:

- Definition: Organizing thoughts and ideas in a logical and coherent manner.

- Importance: A well-structured message is easier to follow and comprehend. It helps the listener grasp the main points and the intended flow of information.

12. Respect:

- Definition: Treating others with courtesy and consideration during communication.

- Importance: Respectful communication builds positive relationships. It fosters an atmosphere of collaboration and encourages open and honest exchanges of ideas.

By incorporating these essential elements into verbal communication, individuals can enhance their ability to convey messages effectively, establish rapport and ensure mutual understanding between speakers and listeners.

Practical tips and exercises to help improve your verbal communication skills:

1. Active Listening Exercises:

- Tip: Practice active listening by giving your full attention to the speaker without interrupting.

- Exercise: Engage in conversations where you focus solely on understanding the speaker's message. Summarize what you've heard to ensure comprehension.

2. Pronunciation and Articulation:

- Tip: Work on your pronunciation and articulation for clarity.

- Exercise: Pronounce tongue twisters and challenging words slowly and clearly. Record yourself and listen for any areas of improvement.

3. Public Speaking Practice:

- Tip: Build confidence through public speaking opportunities.

- Exercise: Start with small group discussions and gradually progress to more formal presentations. Seek constructive feedback to refine your delivery.

4. Expand Vocabulary:

- Tip: Enhance your vocabulary for more effective communication.

- Exercise: Learn a new word each day and incorporate it into your conversations. Use synonyms to express ideas in different ways.

5. Role-Playing Scenarios:

- Tip: Improve communication in various situations through role-playing.

- Exercise: Create scenarios (job interviews, negotiations etc.) and practice your communication skills with a partner. Focus on maintaining poise and clarity.

6. Use of Mirroring:

- Tip: Establish a connection with others through mirroring.

- Exercise: Mirror the body language and tone of someone you're conversing with. This builds rapport and demonstrates active engagement.

7. Record and Review:

- Tip: Reflect on your verbal communication through self-assessment.

- Exercise: Record yourself speaking on different topics. Review the recordings to identify areas for improvement, such as pacing, tone or filler words.

8. Storytelling Practice:

- Tip: Enhance engagement by becoming a compelling storyteller.

- Exercise: Share personal stories or narratives with friends or family. Focus on maintaining a captivating narrative flow.

9. Visualization Techniques:

- Tip: Picture successful communication scenarios in your mind.

- Exercise: Before important conversations or presentations, visualize yourself speaking confidently and effectively. This mental preparation can boost your actual performance.

10. Join Speaking Groups:

- Tip: Surround yourself with opportunities for communication improvement.

- Exercise: Join public speaking clubs, discussion groups or language exchange meetups. Regularly participating in these groups exposes you to diverse communication styles.

11. Monitor Your Pace:

- Tip: Be mindful of your speaking pace for better comprehension.

- Exercise: Practice slowing down your speech. Use pauses strategically to emphasize key points and allow listeners to absorb information.

12. Expand Cultural Awareness:

- Tip: Learn about and respect cultural differences in communication.

- Exercise: Engage in conversations with people from different cultural backgrounds. Pay attention to cultural differences in communication styles and adapt accordingly.

13. Use Feedback Constructively:

- Tip: Seek feedback to identify areas for improvement.

- Exercise: Ask friends, family or colleagues for constructive feedback on your communication. Use their insights to refine your skills.

14. Mindful Breathing:

- Tip: Manage anxiety and stress for clearer communication.

- Exercise: Practice mindful breathing exercises to stay calm and focused before important conversations or presentations.

15. Expression Exercises:

- Tip: Work on clear expression for improved understanding.

- Exercise: Practice voicing each syllable clearly. Repeat challenging words and focus on crisp pronunciation.

Consistent practice of these tips and exercises can contribute to significant improvement in your verbal communication skills over time. Remember that effective communication is an ongoing learning process and each opportunity to communicate provides a chance for growth.

Benefits of Developing Strong Verbal Communication Skills for Students:

---

1. Academic Success:

- Highlight: Strong verbal communication skills contribute to effective class participation, enabling students to articulate their thoughts clearly during discussions, presentations and group activities. This engagement often translates to improved academic performance.

2. Enhanced Learning Experience:

- Highlight: Clear communication with teachers and peers facilitates a better understanding of course materials. Students who can express their questions and ideas effectively are more likely to receive constructive feedback and support, leading to a more enriching learning experience.

3. Confidence Building:

- Highlight: Developing strong verbal communication skills instills confidence in students. The ability to express oneself with assurance fosters self-esteem, making students more willing to actively participate in various academic and social settings.

4. Career Readiness:

- Highlight: Verbal communication is a vital skill in the professional world. Students who develop effective communication skills are better prepared for job interviews, workplace interactions and collaboration with colleagues, giving them a competitive edge in their future careers.

5. Critical Thinking and Problem-Solving:

- Highlight: Articulating thoughts verbally encourages critical thinking. Students who can express their ideas verbally are more likely to engage in thoughtful discussions, analyze information critically and present well-reasoned arguments.

6. Building Relationships:

- Highlight: Strong verbal communication skills contribute to the development of positive relationships with peers, teachers and mentors. Students who can express themselves clearly are often perceived as approachable and are more likely to form meaningful connections within their academic community.

7. Effective Teamwork:

- Highlight: Collaboration is a crucial aspect of many academic projects. Students with strong verbal communication skills can contribute effectively to group work, express their ideas and navigate conflicts, fostering a productive and harmonious teamwork environment.

8. Leadership Development:

- Highlight: Verbal communication is a cornerstone of leadership. Students who can communicate persuasively and inspire others are more likely to take on leadership roles, whether in student organizations, extracurricular activities or community initiatives.

9. Presentation Skills:

- Highlight: As students progress academically and professionally, they often encounter situations that require effective presentation skills. Strong verbal communication skills enable students to deliver engaging and impactful presentations, a valuable asset in various settings.

10. Personal Growth:

- Highlight: Verbal communication is not only a tool for academic and professional success but also for personal growth. It allows students to express their feelings, thoughts and aspirations, fostering self-awareness and emotional intelligence.

11. Networking Opportunities:

- Highlight: Building a professional network begins with effective communication. Students who can articulate their goals, express their interests and engage in meaningful conversations are more likely to leverage networking opportunities for internships, mentorships and career advancement.

12. Global Awareness:

- Highlight: In an interconnected world, strong verbal communication skills enable students to communicate across cultural and linguistic boundaries. This promotes global awareness, tolerance and the ability to collaborate with individuals from diverse backgrounds.

13. Advocacy and Activism:

- Highlight: Students with strong verbal communication skills can advocate for causes they believe in. Whether expressing opinions in debates, writing persuasive essays or participating in activism, effective communication amplifies their voice and impact.

14. Life-long Learning:

- Highlight: Verbal communication is integral to the exchange of ideas and information. Students who develop strong communication skills are better equipped for a life-long journey of learning, adapting and effectively conveying their evolving understanding of the world.

15. Cultivating Empathy:

- Highlight: Verbal communication is a gateway to understanding others. Students who can express empathy and actively listen to their peers develop strong interpersonal skills, contributing to a compassionate and inclusive academic environment.

In summary, strong verbal communication skills empower students academically, professionally and personally, preparing them for a future where effective communication is a key determinant of success in various aspects of life.

Non-Verbal Communication Skills

In the realm of personality development for students, effective communication skills play a crucial role. While verbal communication is often emphasized, non-verbal communication skills are equally important and often overlooked. Non-verbal signs can greatly impact how others perceive us and can make or break our interpersonal relationships. This chapter aims to shed light on the significance of non-verbal communication skills and provide practical tips for students, parents, teachers and trainers to foster better communication.

Non-verbal communication encompasses body language, facial expressions, gestures, tone of voice and personal space. These forms of expression can convey emotions, attitudes and intentions, often surpassing the power of words alone. Students who master non-verbal communication skills can enhance their self-confidence, build stronger relationships and improve their overall personality development.

For students, understanding and utilizing non-verbal cues can be a game-changer in various social settings. Whether it's a job interview, a presentation or a classroom discussion, non-verbal communication can influence how others perceive their competence and credibility. Parents, teachers and trainers also play a vital role in helping students develop these skills. By providing guidance and creating environments that encourage open communication, they can help students navigate social situations with ease.

To enhance non-verbal communication skills, students can start by becoming more aware of their own body language and facial expressions. They can practice maintaining eye contact, using appropriate hand gestures and adopting a confident posture. Additionally, understanding cultural differences in non-verbal communication is crucial in an increasingly diverse world.

Parents, teachers and trainers can support students by organizing workshops or training sessions focused on non-verbal communication. These sessions can provide practical exercises, role-plays and discussions to help students develop a better understanding of non-verbal cues and their impact.

Furthermore, incorporating non-verbal communication skills into the curriculum can benefit students in the long run. By incorporating activities such as group discussions, role-plays and presentations, teachers can create opportunities for students to practice and improve their non-verbal communication skills.

In conclusion, non-verbal communication skills are an essential aspect of personality development for students. By understanding and honing these skills, students can become effective communicators, fostering better relationships and achieving success in various aspects of their lives. Parents, teachers and trainers have a crucial role to play in guiding and supporting students in their journey towards mastering non-verbal communication skills. By fostering an environment that encourages open communication and providing practical training, we can help students become skilled communicators who are well-equipped for the challenges of the future.

Active Listening and Empathy

In today's fast-paced world, effective communication skills are essential for success in both personal and professional relationships. One crucial aspect of communication is active listening and empathy. These skills not only enhance our understanding of others but also enable us to build strong and meaningful connections with them. This chapter will explore the importance of active listening and empathy in personality development for students.

Active listening is the ability to fully concentrate on and comprehend a speaker's message. It involves not only hearing the words but also understanding the speaker's emotions, intentions and underlying meaning. By practising active listening, students can improve their communication skills, foster better relationships and gain a deeper understanding of others.

Empathy, on the other hand, refers to the ability to understand and share the feelings of another person. It involves stepping into someone else's shoes and seeing the world from their perspective. Empathy helps students develop compassion, kindness and a genuine interest in others. It allows them to connect on a deeper level, resolve conflicts peacefully and become more inclusive and accepting individuals.

For students, active listening and empathy have numerous benefits. Firstly, these skills foster better relationships with peers, teachers and family members. By actively listening and empathizing, students can build trust, enhance cooperation and create a positive learning environment. Moreover, these skills enable students to resolve conflicts effectively and respectfully, promoting harmony and understanding among their peers.

Additionally, active listening and empathy contribute to personal growth. Students who practice active listening are more likely to grasp information accurately, make informed decisions and perform better academically. Furthermore, empathy cultivates emotional intelligence, which is essential for self-awareness, self-management and social awareness.

To develop active listening and empathy skills, students, parents, teachers and trainers can employ various strategies. These include maintaining eye contact, asking clarifying questions, summarizing the speaker's message and validating the speaker's feelings. Additionally, individuals can participate in role-playing activities, engage in open-minded discussions and practice mindfulness to enhance their listening and empathy skills.

In conclusion, active listening and empathy are indispensable skills for students' personality development.

By honing these skills, students can improve their communication abilities, build meaningful relationships and foster personal growth. The cultivation of active listening and empathy not only benefits students but also creates a positive and harmonious environment in schools, families and society as a whole.

Key Takeaways:

- Good communication involves speaking, listening and understanding others.
- Clear communication builds stronger relationships and reduces misunderstandings.

Call to Action Exercises:

For Students:

1. **Active Listening Practice**: Spend time each day practising active listening with friends or family.
2. **Speech Reflection**: Record yourself speaking on a topic and reflect on areas for improvement.
3. **Non-Verbal Communication**: Try expressing yourself through body language alone in a simple activity.

For Parents:

1. **Model Good Listening**: Show attentive listening in conversations with your child.
2. **Encourage Open Dialogue**: Ask open-ended questions to get your child talking freely.

3. **Family Discussion**: Dedicate time to discuss a topic together as a family, practising respectful communication.

For Teachers/Trainers:

1. **Role-Playing Activity**: Set up role-play exercises that allow students to practice communication skills.
2. **Feedback Exercise**: Provide constructive feedback on their communication.
3. **Group Projects**: Arrange group work to encourage communication and collaboration.

Chapter 6: Developing Emotional Intelligence

Understanding Emotional Intelligence

Emotional intelligence is a vital aspect of personality development for students. In this chapter, we will explore the core components of emotional intelligence, its relevance in personal and academic growth and practical strategies to enhance it.

Emotional intelligence refers to the ability to recognize, understand and manage our own emotions while also being aware of others' emotions. It involves skills such as self-awareness, self-regulation, empathy and effective communication. Research has shown that emotional intelligence plays a significant role in various aspects of life, including academic success, social relationships and overall well-being.

For students, emotional intelligence is particularly crucial as it affects their ability to cope with stress, handle conflicts and navigate social interactions. By developing emotional intelligence, students can better understand and manage their own emotions, leading to improved self-esteem and resilience. Additionally, it enables them to empathize with others, build meaningful relationships and work collaboratively, which are essential skills for success in school and beyond.

To enhance emotional intelligence, students can start by cultivating self-awareness. This involves recognizing and understanding their own emotions, strengths and weaknesses. Journaling, mindfulness exercises and reflection can be helpful practices to develop self-awareness. Students should also focus on self-regulation, which involves managing their emotions and impulses effectively. Learning techniques such as deep breathing and positive self-talk can aid in self-regulation.

Empathy is another crucial aspect of emotional intelligence. Students should strive to understand and appreciate the perspectives and feelings of others. Engaging in active listening, seeking feedback and practising kindness can foster empathy. Effective communication skills are also vital for emotional intelligence. Students should learn to express themselves assertively, actively listen to others and resolve conflicts constructively.

Parents, teachers and trainers play a significant role in supporting students' emotional intelligence development. They can create a safe and nurturing environment that encourages open communication and emotional expression. Promoting social and emotional learning programs in schools can also provide valuable tools and resources for students to develop emotional intelligence.

In conclusion, understanding emotional intelligence is essential for students' personality development. By cultivating skills such as self-awareness, self-regulation, empathy and effective communication, students can enhance their emotional intelligence, leading to improved personal and academic growth. With the support of parents, teachers and trainers, students can develop strong emotional intelligence foundations that will benefit them throughout their lives.

Managing and Expressing Emotions

Emotions play a vital role in our lives, shaping our thoughts, actions and relationships. Understanding how to manage and express our emotions is a fundamental aspect of personality development for students. This chapter aims to provide valuable insights and practical strategies for students, parents, teachers and trainers to nurture emotional intelligence and build strong foundations for personal growth.

For students, learning to manage emotions is crucial for overall well-being and academic success. By recognizing and understanding their emotions, students can effectively cope with stress, handle conflicts and develop resilience. This chapter will explore various techniques such as mindfulness, deep breathing exercises and journaling that students can incorporate into their daily routine to regulate their emotions. Additionally, it will emphasize the importance of seeking support from trusted adults or counselors when experiencing complex emotions.

Parents play an instrumental role in helping their children navigate their emotional landscape. This chapter will guide parents in fostering open communication, active listening and empathy within the family. It will highlight the significance of modeling healthy emotional expression and providing a safe space for children to share their feelings.

Parents will also gain insights into recognizing signs of emotional distress and implementing strategies to support their children's emotional well-being.

Teachers and trainers have a unique opportunity to shape students' emotional development within the classroom environment. This chapter will emphasize the importance of creating a positive and inclusive atmosphere where students feel comfortable expressing their emotions. Teachers will gain insights into effective communication techniques, conflict resolution strategies and promoting emotional intelligence through activities and discussions. It will also address the significance of self-care for educators and provide practical techniques to manage their own emotions within the demanding school environment.

By addressing the niche of personality development for students, this chapter aims to equip students, parents, teachers and trainers with the necessary tools to enhance emotional intelligence. Understanding emotions, managing them effectively and expressing them in a healthy manner are essential skills for personal growth and success in various aspects of life. By integrating these strategies into their routines, individuals will be better equipped to navigate challenges, build meaningful relationships and lead fulfilling lives.

Empathy and Emotional Awareness

In today's fast-paced world, it is more important than ever for students to develop strong interpersonal skills. One of the key aspects of personality development is the ability to empathize and be emotionally aware. This chapter will delve into the significance of empathy and emotional awareness in building strong foundations for students.

Empathy is the ability to understand and share the feelings of others. It is the foundation of meaningful relationships and effective communication. When students develop empathy, they become more agreed to the emotions and needs of those around them, fostering a sense of connection and understanding. By putting themselves in someone else's shoes, students can gain a deeper insight into different perspectives and experiences, thus nurturing their interpersonal skills.

Emotional awareness, on the other hand, involves recognizing and understanding one's own emotions. It is about being able to identify and manage feelings effectively. When students are emotionally aware, they can regulate their emotions, make informed decisions and maintain healthy relationships. Moreover, emotional awareness helps students to understand the impact their actions and words have on others, nurturing empathy and compassion.

Developing empathy and emotional awareness requires practice and self-reflection. Students can engage in activities that encourage them to step into different roles and perspectives, such as role-playing or storytelling exercises. These activities help them develop a deeper understanding of diverse emotions and experiences. Additionally, encouraging students to journal or keep a feelings diary can help them become more aware of their own emotions and triggers.

Parents, teachers and trainers play a crucial role in nurturing empathy and emotional awareness in students. By modeling empathetic behaviour and creating a safe and supportive environment, they can encourage students to express their emotions and validate their experiences. Open discussions about emotions, empathy and the importance of understanding others can also help students develop these vital skills.

In conclusion, empathy and emotional awareness are essential components of personality development for students. By cultivating these skills, students can build strong foundations for lasting relationships, effective communication and personal growth. Students, parents, teachers and trainers need to recognize the significance of empathy and emotional awareness and actively engage in activities and discussions that promote their development.

Valuable Insights and Practical Strategies for Nurturing Emotional Intelligence in Students, Parents, Teachers and Trainers:

For Students:

Insights:

Understanding Emotions:

Emotions are like colours on a canvas, making life interesting and vibrant. Each emotion, whether it's happiness, sadness or excitement, is a piece of the puzzle that helps us understand ourselves better.

Practical Strategies:

1. Emotion Check-Ins:

Take a few minutes each day to check in on your feelings. Use a feelings chart or draw your own emotions to express how you feel. This helps you become more aware of your emotions and why you might be feeling a certain way.

2. Expressing Emotions:

Share your feelings with someone you trust. It could be a friend, a family member or a teacher. You can also express your emotions through art, writing or simply talking. It's like letting the sunshine out from inside you!

3. Empathy Building:

Imagine how your friend feels when they are happy or sad. Practice active listening by nodding and showing that you understand. Being a good friend means caring about how others feel.

4. Mindfulness Moments:

Expansion: Mindfulness is like taking a mental break. Find a quiet spot, close your eyes and take a few deep breaths. Focus on your breath and let go of any worries. It's a mini-vacation for your mind!

For Parents:

Insights:

Parental Influence:

Parents are like emotional superheroes for their kids. Children learn about feelings by watching how parents handle their own emotions. Parents have the power to shape a child's emotional world.

Practical Strategies:

1. Open Communication:

Create a cozy space where your child feels comfortable talking about their feelings. Listen without interrupting and let them know it's okay to feel any emotion. Your love is like a safe harbour for their emotions.

2. Modeling Emotional Regulation:

Show your child how to handle stress or frustration in a healthy way. Take a deep breath when you feel upset or share your feelings with them. Your actions are like a guidebook for managing emotions.

3. Empathy Activities:

Engage in activities that teach empathy, like reading stories together. Discuss the characters' emotions and relate them to real-life situations. Being in someone else's shoes helps us understand them better.

4. Teaching Emotional Vocabulary:

Introduce new emotion words to your child. Use simple language to help them express how they feel. For example, say, "I can see you're really excited about your day!" This builds their emotional vocabulary.

For Teachers:

Insights:

Classroom Emotional Atmosphere:

Imagine the classroom as an emotional garden. The atmosphere you create impacts how students feel and learn.

A positive and supportive environment is like fertile soil for emotional growth.

Practical Strategies:

1. Emotion Check-Ins:

Start the day with a quick emotional check-in. It's like taking attendance but for feelings! This helps students share how they're doing and creates a caring atmosphere in the classroom.

2. Conflict Resolution Skills:

Teach students how to solve problems peacefully. Create a "Peace Corner" in the classroom where students can go to talk and find solutions together. This helps them become emotional problem-solvers.

3. Emotion-Focused Lessons:

Expansion: Bring emotions into your lessons. When reading a story, discuss how the characters might feel. Use real-life examples to explore emotions and problem-solving. Learning becomes more exciting when emotions are part of the journey.

4. Mindfulness in the Classroom:

Integrate short mindfulness exercises into the day. It could be a few minutes of deep breathing or a mindful moment before a test. Mindfulness helps students stay calm and focused, like a mental reset button.

For Trainers:

Insights:

Impact on Learning Environment:

Trainers are like emotional architects, designing the learning atmosphere. Building emotional intelligence enhances the overall training experience, creating a space where participants can learn and grow.

Practical Strategies:

1. Creating a Supportive Environment:

Foster a training environment where everyone feels supported and included. Encourage participants to share their thoughts and feelings openly. This creates a positive space for learning and collaboration.

2. Interactive Activities:

Include activities that promote self-awareness and empathy. Interactive exercises, role-playing or group discussions help participants practice emotional intelligence skills. Learning becomes more engaging when everyone actively participates.

3. Feedback with Empathy:

When providing feedback, use empathy and understanding. Acknowledge participants' efforts and offer guidance for improvement. A supportive feedback approach helps build trust and motivates participants to grow.

4. Cultivating Emotional Resilience:

Discuss the importance of resilience in the training. Share stories of challenges and how they were overcome. Cultivating emotional resilience prepares participants for the ups and downs of their learning journey.

In embracing these insights and implementing these practical strategies, we create a foundation for emotional intelligence, fostering personal growth in students, parents, teachers and trainers alike. It's like planting seeds of emotional wisdom that will continue to bloom throughout life's journey.

Key Takeaways:

- Emotional intelligence helps in understanding and managing emotions, improving social interactions.
- It involves self-awareness, empathy and emotional regulation, which enhance personal and professional relationships.

Call to Action Exercises:

For Students:

1. **Emotion Diary**: Write down daily emotions and analyze what caused them.
2. **Empathy Practice**: Take time to understand a friend's point of view on an issue.
3. **Breathing Techniques**: Practice deep breathing to stay calm when emotions run high.

For Parents:

1. **Discuss Emotions**: Have open conversations about emotions with your child, validating their feelings.
2. **Model Empathy**: Show empathy in daily interactions to teach emotional awareness.

3. **Emotion Labeling**: Help your child identify and name their emotions in various situations.

For Teachers/Trainers:

1. **Emotion Vocabulary Exercise**: Teach students words to describe different emotions.
2. **Group Reflection**: Encourage students to share feelings about a recent project or activity.
3. **Mindfulness Activity**: Lead a brief mindfulness session to help students regulate their emotions.

Chapter 7
Cultivating Positive Relationships

The Role of Relationships in Personality Development

Introduction:

In the journey of personality development, relationships play a crucial role. Our interactions with others, whether it be with friends, family members, teachers or even acquaintances, shape our personalities in significant ways. This chapter will explore the deep impact that relationships have on personality development, providing valuable insights for students, parents, teachers and trainers who are invested in fostering personal growth and well-being.

1. Influence of Family Relationships:

Family is the foundation upon which our personalities are built. The dynamics we experience within our families profoundly impact our development. The support, values and communication styles within a family shape our sense of self, self-confidence and ability to form healthy relationships outside the family unit.

2. Friendships and Peer Relationships:

As students, the friendships we cultivate during our school years greatly influence our personality development. Peer relationships provide opportunities for socialization, empathy and understanding. They help us learn important life skills such as conflict resolution, teamwork and compromise. Additionally, friendships can shape our interests, values and aspirations, ultimately influencing the paths we choose in life.

3. Relationships with Teachers:

Teachers play a pivotal role in the personality development of students. Positive relationships with teachers foster a sense of belonging, motivation and self-esteem. A supportive and nurturing teacher-student relationship not only enhances academic performance but also contributes to the overall development of a student's personality.

4. Role of Mentors and Trainers:

Outside the immediate academic environment, mentors and trainers from various fields can have a profound impact on personality development. Whether it is a sports coach, a music teacher or a career mentor, these relationships provide guidance, inspiration and opportunities for personal growth. Mentors and trainers help students discover their strengths, overcome challenges and develop essential life skills.

Conclusion:

In conclusion, relationships play a vital role in the process of personality development for students. From family dynamics to friendships, from teacher-student relationships to mentorship opportunities, the connections we form throughout our lives shape who we become. Students, parents, teachers and trainers must recognize the significance of fostering positive relationships and creating supportive environments that allow for personal growth and the development of well-rounded individuals. Understanding the influence of relationships on personality development is an essential step towards building strong foundations for students' overall well-being and success.

Building Healthy Friendships

Introduction:

Friendships play a crucial role in our lives, especially during our formative years. They shape our personality, influence our choices and contribute to our overall growth and development. In this chapter, we will explore the importance of building healthy friendships and provide useful strategies for students, parents, teachers and trainers to foster positive relationships.

Understanding the Importance of Healthy Friendships:

Healthy friendships have numerous benefits for students. They provide emotional support, boost self-esteem, enhance social skills and create a sense of belonging. Students who have healthy friendships tend to be happier, more motivated and better equipped to handle challenges.

Strategies for Students:

1. Be yourself: Authenticity is key to building healthy friendships. Embrace your unique qualities and interests and find friends who appreciate you for who you are.

2. Choose wisely: Surround yourself with friends who share similar values, goals and aspirations. Seek out individuals who inspire and uplift you.

3. Communicate effectively: Open and honest communication is vital for maintaining healthy friendships. Express your thoughts and feelings clearly, while also being a good listener.

Strategies for Parents:

1. Encourage social activities: Provide opportunities for your child to engage in group activities, clubs or sports where they can interact with peers and build friendships.

2. Teach empathy and kindness: Instill in your child the importance of treating others with respect and empathy. Encourage them to be kind and inclusive towards their friends.

3. Monitor online interactions: In today's digital age, it is crucial to monitor your child's online friendships.

Discuss internet safety, set boundaries and encourage healthy online behaviour.

Strategies for Teachers and Trainers:

1. Foster a supportive environment: Create a classroom or training environment that promotes inclusivity, collaboration and respect. Encourage students to work together and build friendships.

2. Teach conflict resolution skills: Help students develop effective conflict resolution skills, such as active listening, compromise and finding win-win solutions. These skills are essential for maintaining healthy friendships.

3. Offer guidance and support: Be a mentor and guide for students, helping them navigate the complexities of friendships. Provide advice and resources to help them build and maintain healthy relationships.

Conclusion:

Building healthy friendships is a crucial aspect of personality development for students. By understanding the importance of healthy friendships and implementing the strategies outlined in this chapter, students, parents, teachers and trainers can contribute to the growth and well-being of students. Remember, fostering healthy friendships will not only benefit individuals but also contribute to a more harmonious and supportive social environment.

Nurturing Family Relationships

In today's fast-paced world, where everyone is busy chasing their dreams and ambitions, it is easy to overlook the importance of nurturing family relationships. However, strong family bonds are crucial for a student's personality development. Building a strong foundation within the family can provide students with the support and guidance they need to thrive in all aspects of their lives.

Students, parents, teachers and trainers all play a vital role in creating an environment that fosters healthy family relationships. It begins with open and honest communication. Students should feel comfortable discussing their thoughts, concerns and aspirations with their family members. Parents, on the other hand, should actively listen and provide guidance without judgment. Teachers and trainers can also facilitate this process by encouraging students to express themselves and promoting healthy communication within the classroom.

Furthermore, spending quality time together as a family is essential for building strong relationships. In today's digital age, it is easy to get caught up in screens and technology. However, allocating dedicated time for family activities, such as family dinners or game nights, can help strengthen the bond between family members. These activities provide an opportunity for everyone to connect, share stories and create lasting memories.

Another aspect of nurturing family relationships is practising empathy and understanding. Each family member has their own unique perspective and experiences. Students, parents, teachers and trainers should strive to understand and respect each other's viewpoints, even if they differ. Empathy allows for a deeper understanding of one another's needs and promotes a culture of compassion within the family.

Finally, it is important to celebrate each other's successes and support each other during difficult times. Students should feel valued and supported by their family members in their academic and personal endeavours. Parents, teachers and trainers can help students set realistic goals and provide the necessary guidance and encouragement to achieve them.

In conclusion, nurturing family relationships is a fundamental aspect of personality development for students. By fostering open communication, spending quality time together, practising empathy and celebrating each other's successes, students can develop a strong sense of self and thrive in all areas of their lives. It is a collective effort that requires the active participation of students, parents, teachers and trainers. Together, they can build strong foundations that will positively impact students' personality development and overall well-being.

Developing Professional Relationships

In today's interconnected world, the ability to develop and maintain professional relationships is an essential skill for students as they embark on their journey towards personal and professional growth. Building Strong Foundations: Personality Development for Students recognizes the significance of this skill and devotes an entire chapter to exploring the intricacies of developing professional relationships.

Students, Parents, Teachers and Trainers alike will find valuable insights and practical advice within this chapter as it highlights the importance of strong professional relationships and offers guidance on how to cultivate and nurture them effectively.

The chapter begins by emphasizing the significance of professional relationships in various aspects of life. Whether it's building a network of mentors and peers, establishing connections with potential employers or fostering meaningful relationships with colleagues, developing professional relationships can open doors to opportunities and facilitate personal growth.

Next, the chapter delves into the essential qualities that students need to cultivate in order to foster strong professional relationships. It emphasizes the importance of effective communication skills, active listening, empathy and professionalism. Through real-life examples and relatable scenarios, students will gain a deeper understanding of how these qualities contribute to the successful development of professional relationships.

Furthermore, the chapter explores practical strategies for building professional relationships. It offers advice on networking, attending industry events and utilizing social media platforms to connect with professionals in their desired fields. Additionally, it provides guidance on how to approach informational interviews, internships and mentorship opportunities, emphasizing the value of learning from experienced individuals.

To provide a holistic perspective, the chapter also addresses the role of parents, teachers and trainers in supporting students' efforts to develop professional relationships. It offers suggestions for parents on how to encourage their children to engage in extracurricular activities and explore diverse interests. For teachers and trainers, it emphasizes the importance of providing students with opportunities to collaborate, engage in group projects and develop teamwork skills.

By the end of this chapter, students, parents, teachers and trainers will have a comprehensive understanding of the significance of developing professional relationships and the strategies they can employ to cultivate and maintain them effectively. Building Strong Foundations: Personality Development for Students ensures that students are equipped with the necessary skills to navigate the professional world with confidence, ultimately leading to personal and professional success.

Let us discuss some intricacies of Developing Professional Relationships for Personality Development in Students:

Building strong professional relationships is like creating a network of support and opportunities that can shape a student's future. Let's explore the intricacies and offer practical insights for students, highlighting the significance of professional relationships in various aspects of life.

Importance of Professional Relationships for Students:

---

1. Academic Success:

- Insight: Professional relationships with teachers and classmates enhance the learning experience. Collaboration and support from peers and educators contribute to academic success.

- Advice: Actively participate in class discussions, seek help when needed and form study groups to foster positive academic connections.

2. Career Readiness:

- Insight: Professional relationships play a crucial role in preparing students for future careers. Networking with professionals, mentors and industry experts opens doors to valuable opportunities.

- Advice: Attend career fairs, connect with professionals in your field of interest and seek guidance from teachers on career pathways.

3. Personal Growth:

- Insight: Interacting with diverse individuals fosters personal growth. Professional relationships provide exposure to different perspectives, cultures and ideas.

- Advice: Embrace opportunities for teamwork, engage in extracurricular activities and participate in community events to broaden your horizons.

Essential Qualities for Cultivating Strong Professional Relationships:

1. Communication Skills:

-Insight: Effective communication is the foundation of any relationship. Clear and respectful communication builds trust and understanding.

- Advice: Practice active listening, express thoughts clearly and be open to feedback from others.

2. Reliability and Accountability:

- Insight: Reliability and accountability create a positive impression. Meeting commitments and taking responsibility for actions build trust.

- Advice: Fulfill your responsibilities on time, be dependable and admit mistakes while working towards solutions.

3. Empathy and Respect:

- Insight: Empathy and respect strengthen connections. Understanding others' perspectives and treating everyone with respect contribute to positive relationships.

- Advice: Be kind, show empathy in challenging situations and appreciate the diversity of backgrounds and ideas.

4. Adaptability:

- Insight: Flexibility and adaptability are vital in dynamic environments. Adapting to different situations and working styles fosters resilience.

- Advice: Embrace change positively, be open to new ideas and adjust your approach when collaborating with diverse groups.

Practical Strategies for Building Professional Relationships:

1. Networking Opportunities:

- Insight: Actively seek networking opportunities to connect with professionals and peers. Networking enhances visibility and opens doors to mentorship.

- Advice: Attend events, join professional organizations and use online platforms to build and maintain a professional network.

2. Effective Online Presence:

- Insight: In the digital age, an online presence is significant. Maintain a professional online profile and use social media responsibly.

- Advice: Showcase your achievements, engage in positive online discussions and connect with professionals in your field.

3. Mentorship and Guidance:

- Insight: Seek mentorship from teachers, professionals or seniors. A mentor provides valuable guidance and helps navigate challenges.

- Advice: Approach teachers or professionals you admire, express your interest in mentorship and be receptive to their insights.

4. Professional Development Opportunities:

- Insight: Engage in activities that contribute to your professional development. Workshops, seminars and training sessions offer learning and networking opportunities.

- Advice: Attend relevant events, seek out skill-building activities and actively participate in discussions to showcase your enthusiasm for learning.

Role of Parents, Teachers and Trainers:

1. Parental Support:

- Insight: Parents play a crucial role in shaping a student's understanding of professional relationships. Encouragement and guidance at home create a positive foundation.

- Advice: Parents can discuss the importance of networking, provide insights into their own professional experiences and support extracurricular activities that enhance interpersonal skills.

2. Teacher Guidance:

- Insight: Teachers act as mentors and guides. They contribute to students' professional development by providing insights into career paths and fostering a positive classroom environment.

- Advice: Teachers can incorporate real-world examples into lessons, facilitate networking opportunities and offer career guidance to students.

3. Trainer Assistance:

- Insight: Trainers in specialized fields can provide practical insights and industry knowledge. They contribute to students' understanding of professional expectations.

- Advice: Trainers can organize workshops, invite guest speakers and provide resources to enhance students' professional skills.

In summary, developing strong professional relationships is a key aspect of personality development for students. By cultivating essential qualities, leveraging practical strategies and receiving support from parents, teachers and trainers, students can build a robust foundation for personal and professional growth. Remember, these relationships are bridges to future opportunities and personal success.

Key Takeaways:

- Positive relationships are built on trust, respect and effective communication.
- Strong connections enhance well-being and provide support during challenges.

Call to Action Exercises:

For Students:

1. **Friendship List**: List qualities you value in a friend and assess if you embody these qualities.
2. **Positive Interactions**: Set a goal to show kindness to someone daily.
3. **Conflict Resolution**: Practice solving a disagreement with a friend in a calm, respectful way.

For Parents:

1. **Encourage Social Activities**: Create opportunities for your child to make friends.
2. **Discuss Respect**: Talk about the importance of respecting others' boundaries.

3. **Model Healthy Relationships**: Demonstrate positive behaviors in your own relationships.

For Teachers/Trainers:

1. **Group Bonding Activities**: Organize activities to help students build stronger relationships.
2. **Classroom Rules on Respect**: Set and enforce rules promoting respect and kindness.
3. **Conflict Resolution Role-Play**: Guide students in role-playing to handle conflicts constructively.

Chapter 8
Time Management and Productivity

The Value of Time Management for Students

In the fast-paced world we live in, time management has become an essential skill for success, especially for students. As students, you are constantly juggling multiple tasks – attending classes, completing assignments, studying for exams, participating in extracurricular activities and maintaining a social life. With so much to do and limited time available, the ability to manage your time effectively becomes crucial.

Time management is not just about getting things done; it is about using your time in a way that aligns with your goals and priorities. By managing your time effectively, you gain control over your schedule, reduce stress, improve productivity and ultimately achieve better results academically and personally.

One of the key benefits of time management for students is improved academic performance. When you allocate specific time slots for studying, you are able to focus better and absorb information more effectively. By avoiding procrastination and setting realistic deadlines, you can complete assignments and projects well in advance, allowing for revisions and improving the quality of your work. Effective time management also enables you to balance your academic commitments with extracurricular activities, ensuring a well-rounded development.

Moreover, time management skills play a significant role in personal growth and development. By prioritizing your tasks, you can allocate time for self-care activities such as exercise, hobbies and relaxation. Taking breaks and rejuvenating yourself helps maintain a healthy work-life balance, reduces burnout and improves overall well-being.

As parents and teachers, it is essential to instill time management skills in students from an early age. By teaching them the value of time and providing them with tools and techniques to manage it effectively, you empower them to take control of their lives and become more responsible individuals. Encouraging students to create daily or weekly schedules, set goals and track their progress fosters a sense of discipline and accountability.

For trainers and educators specializing in personality development for students, incorporating time management techniques in their curriculum can be highly beneficial. By integrating interactive exercises and workshops on time management, trainers can help students develop organizational skills, prioritize tasks and manage their time efficiently.

In conclusion, time management is an invaluable skill for students, parents, teachers and trainers alike. By mastering this skill, students can achieve academic success, personal growth and a sense of control over their lives. So, make time management a priority and start building strong foundations for a successful future.

Techniques for Effective Time Management

In today's world, effective time management is a crucial skill for students to develop. It not only helps them stay organized and focused but also allows them to make the most of their abilities and potential. This chapter explores various techniques that can be employed to improve time management skills, ensuring that students can build strong foundations for personality development.

1. Prioritization:

One of the key techniques for effective time management is prioritization. Students need to identify their most important tasks and allocate time accordingly. By setting priorities, they can complete essential tasks first, ensuring they do not get overwhelmed or miss deadlines.

2. Setting Clear Goals:

Setting clear and realistic goals is another essential aspect of effective time management. Students should develop a clear understanding of what they want to achieve and break these goals into smaller, manageable tasks. This approach allows for better planning and ensures that time is utilized efficiently.

3. Creating a Schedule:

Developing a schedule is a vital tool for effective time management. Students should allocate specific time slots for different activities throughout the day, including academic work, extracurricular activities and leisure time. A well-structured schedule helps students stay on track and avoid wasting time.

4. Avoiding Procrastination:

Procrastination can be a significant obstacle to effective time management. Students need to learn to recognize when they are putting off important tasks and develop strategies to overcome this habit. By breaking larger tasks into smaller, more manageable parts and setting deadlines, students can maintain focus and complete tasks in a timely manner.

5. Time Blocking:

Time blocking is a technique that involves dedicating specific time blocks to particular activities. By grouping similar tasks together, students can improve productivity and avoid constant switching between different activities. This technique helps students maintain focus and improve efficiency.

6. Delegation and Saying No:

Learning to delegate tasks and say no when necessary is crucial for effective time management. Students should recognize their limitations and avoid taking on more than they can handle. Delegating tasks to others or politely declining requests that do not align with their goals allows students to prioritize their time effectively.

Effective time management is a valuable skill that contributes to the overall development of students. By implementing these techniques, students can build strong foundations for personality development. Parents, teachers and trainers play a vital role in guiding students in mastering these techniques and ensuring they have the necessary tools to manage their time effectively. With improved time management skills, students can achieve their goals, reduce stress and enjoy a balanced and fulfilling academic and personal life.

Enhancing Productivity and Avoiding Procrastination

In today's world, students must develop strong foundations in order to excel academically and personally. One key aspect of building these foundations is enhancing productivity and avoiding the common trap of procrastination. This chapter aims to provide students, parents, teachers and trainers with valuable insights and effective strategies to cultivate productivity and overcome procrastination.

Productivity is not simply about getting things done; it is about utilizing time and resources efficiently to achieve desired results. However, many students struggle with managing their time effectively, leading to wasted opportunities and increased stress levels. By understanding the importance of time management and adopting practical techniques, students can significantly enhance their productivity.

One effective strategy is to prioritize tasks based on urgency and importance. This helps students focus on the most critical assignments and prevents them from getting overwhelmed by non-essential tasks. Additionally, breaking larger tasks into smaller, more manageable chunks allows for a sense of progress and accomplishment, boosting motivation along the way.

Another crucial aspect of productivity is maintaining a healthy work-life balance. Students often neglect their personal well-being in pursuit of academic success, which can lead to burnout and decreased overall performance. Encouraging students to set aside time for relaxation, hobbies and social activities promotes mental and emotional well-being, ultimately enhancing productivity.

However, even with effective time management techniques in place, procrastination can still creep in and hinder progress. Procrastination is a common challenge faced by students, often stemming from feelings of overwhelm, fear of failure or a lack of motivation. By understanding the underlying causes of procrastination, students can develop strategies to overcome it.

One powerful technique is to break tasks into smaller, more manageable steps and set specific deadlines for each step. This creates a sense of urgency and makes tasks appear less scary. Additionally, implementing accountability measures, such as sharing goals with a trusted friend or using productivity apps, can help students stay on track and avoid falling into the procrastination trap.

Through adopting these strategies and cultivating a productivity mindset, students can build strong foundations for success. However, parents, teachers and trainers need to support and guide students in this journey. By providing resources, mentorship and regular check-ins, they can help students develop the necessary skills to enhance productivity and avoid procrastination.

In conclusion, enhancing productivity and avoiding procrastination are essential aspects of personality development for students. By implementing effective time management techniques, maintaining a healthy work-life balance and overcoming procrastination, students can unlock their full potential and achieve success in all areas of their lives.

Key Takeaways:

- Effective time management is essential for balancing responsibilities and achieving goals.
- Good productivity habits help maximize time and reduce stress.

Call to Action Exercises:

For Students:

1. **Daily Planner**: Write a daily schedule to manage study, play and rest time.
2. **Prioritization Exercise**: List tasks by importance and complete them in order.
3. **Set Breaks**: Take short breaks between study sessions for better focus.

For Parents:

1. **Time-Blocking Together**: Help your child allocate time for homework, tasks and relaxation.
2. **Encourage a Routine**: Set consistent times for homework and rest to build structure.

3. **Avoid Over-Scheduling**: Allow free time so your child learns self-management.

For Teachers/Trainers:

1. **Class Schedule**: Teach students how to create a weekly schedule for their studies.
2. **Task List Exercise**: Encourage students to create and follow daily task lists.
3. **Time Awareness**: Give timed tasks to improve students' focus and time estimation.

Chapter 9
Resilience and Stress Management

Developing Resilience in Students

Resilience is a fundamental trait that every individual should possess in order to navigate through life's challenges and setbacks. In the book "Building Strong Foundations: Personality Development for Students," we delve into the topic of developing resilience in students, providing insights and practical strategies for students, parents, teachers and trainers.

Resilience is not an innate quality; it is a skill that can be cultivated and strengthened. By developing resilience, students can effectively cope with stress, bounce back from failures and adapt to new situations. This chapter offers a comprehensive understanding of resilience and its significance in the context of personality development for students.

For students, this chapter provides valuable insights into the importance of resilience and offers practical tools to enhance their resilience levels. They will learn to develop a growth mindset, which enables them to view challenges as opportunities for growth rather than obstacles. Additionally, students will discover the power of self-belief and positive self-talk as essential components of resilience.

Parents play a crucial role in nurturing resilience in their children. This chapter provides guidance to parents on fostering resilience in their children's lives. Parents will learn effective communication strategies, how to encourage problem-solving skills and the importance of providing a supportive environment. By nurturing resilience in their children, parents can equip them with the tools to face life's challenges head-on.

Teachers and trainers have a unique opportunity to instill resilience in students through their teaching methods. This chapter offers valuable insights and practical techniques for educators to integrate resilience-building practices into their classrooms. Teachers will explore the importance of creating a safe and inclusive learning environment, fostering a growth mindset and providing opportunities for students to develop problem-solving skills.

In conclusion, the chapter "Developing Resilience in Students" from the book "Building Strong Foundations: Personality Development for Students" is a valuable resource for students, parents, teachers and trainers. It delves into the significance of resilience in the context of personality development and offers practical strategies to cultivate resilience in students. By developing resilience, students will be equipped with the tools to navigate life's challenges, bounce back from setbacks and thrive in an ever-changing world.

Coping with Stress and Pressure

In today's fast-paced world, students are often faced with various stressors and pressures that can affect their well-being, performance and overall personality development. It is crucial for students, parents, teachers and trainers to understand and address these challenges effectively. This chapter on "Coping with Stress and Pressure" aims to provide valuable insights and practical strategies to navigate through these difficulties and build a strong foundation for personality development.

Stress and pressure can arise from numerous sources, such as academic expectations, social interactions, extracurricular activities and personal relationships. Recognizing and acknowledging these stress factors is the first step towards coping with them. Students need to understand that experiencing stress is normal and that everyone encounters it at some point. By accepting this fact, students can shift their mindset to focus on developing resilience and effective coping mechanisms.

One effective strategy to manage stress is by developing healthy lifestyle habits. Regular exercise, a balanced diet and sufficient sleep contribute to physical and mental well-being, fostering a more resilient mindset. Additionally, students can benefit from practicing relaxation techniques like deep breathing exercises, meditation or engaging in hobbies and activities that bring them joy and relaxation.

Moreover, effective time management is essential in coping with stress and pressure. Students should learn to prioritize tasks, set realistic goals and create a well-structured schedule that allows for breaks and self-care. By managing their time efficiently, students can avoid last-minute panic and reduce unnecessary stress.

Another crucial aspect of coping with stress is building a support system. Students should be encouraged to communicate their feelings and concerns with trusted friends, family members, teachers or trainers who can provide guidance and support. Additionally, schools and educational institutions should establish counseling services to provide professional help when necessary.

It is equally important for parents, teachers and trainers to create a supportive environment that encourages open communication and fosters a positive mindset. By understanding the challenges students face, adults can provide guidance, encouragement and motivation; ultimately contributing to their overall personality development.

In conclusion, coping with stress and pressure is an essential skill for students to develop as they navigate through their educational journey. By adopting strategies such as healthy lifestyle habits, effective time management and building a support system, students can build a strong foundation for their personality development. Furthermore, it is crucial for parents, teachers and trainers to play an active role in creating a supportive environment that facilitates the growth and well-being of students. With these tools and support, students can thrive academically, emotionally and socially.

Strategies for Maintaining a Balanced Lifestyle

In today's fast-paced world, where students are often juggling multiple responsibilities and facing increasing pressure, maintaining a balanced lifestyle is crucial for their overall well-being and success. This chapter explores various strategies that can help students achieve a harmonious balance between their academic, personal and social lives.

1. Prioritize and set realistic goals: Start by identifying your priorities and setting achievable goals. Understand that you cannot excel in every aspect of your life simultaneously. Instead, focus on a few key areas and allocate your time and energy accordingly. This will help you avoid feeling overwhelmed and allow you to make steady progress.

2. Time management: Effectively managing your time is essential for maintaining balance. Create a schedule or use productivity apps to allocate specific time slots for studying, extracurricular activities, relaxation and socializing. Stick to the schedule as much as possible, but also allow flexibility for unexpected events or relaxation.

3. Practice self-care: Taking care of your physical, mental and emotional well-being is crucial for maintaining balance. Make sure to get enough sleep, eat a nutritious diet and engage in regular exercise. Additionally, practice stress-relief techniques like

meditation, deep breathing or engaging in hobbies that bring you joy.

4. Cultivate healthy relationships: Surround yourself with positive and supportive individuals who uplift and motivate you. Maintain open communication with your friends, parents and teachers to foster healthy relationships. Building a strong support system will not only help you manage stress but also provide emotional stability and encouragement.

5. Learn to say no: It's important to recognize your limits and not take on more than you can handle. Learn to say no to activities or commitments that will overwhelm you or hinder your ability to maintain balance. Prioritize your well-being and understand that it is okay to decline certain opportunities or obligations.

6. Seek guidance and support: Reach out to your parents, teachers or trainers for guidance and support when needed. They can offer valuable advice, help you prioritize and provide insights on achieving a balanced lifestyle. Don't hesitate to seek professional help if you are struggling with stress, anxiety or any other mental health concerns.

By implementing these strategies, students can establish and maintain a balanced lifestyle that will contribute to their overall well-being and success. Remember, achieving balance is an ongoing process that requires consistent effort and self-reflection. With time and practice, you will find a healthy equilibrium that allows you to prosper academically, personally and socially.

Key Takeaways:

- Resilience helps individuals cope with setbacks and grow stronger.
- Effective stress management reduces anxiety and improves emotional health.

Call to Action Exercises:

For Students:

1. **Gratitude Practice**: List three things you're grateful for each day.
2. **Stress-Relief Techniques**: Try techniques like deep breathing or journaling during stressful moments.
3. **Self-Care**: Dedicate time each week to activities that relax and recharge you.

For Parents:

1. **Encourage Healthy Coping**: Teach your child stress-relief techniques such as journaling or exercise.

2. **Model Resilience**: Share stories of overcoming challenges in your own life.
3. **Praise Effort, Not Just Results**: Reinforce resilience by focusing on the effort put in.

For Teachers/Trainers:

1. **Resilience Stories**: Share stories of resilient individuals to inspire students.
2. **Teach Relaxation Techniques**: Lead a short relaxation session at the end of the day.
3. **Positive Reframing**: Encourage students to view mistakes as learning opportunities.

Chapter 10
Personal Values and Ethics

Understanding Personal Values and Ethics

In the journey of personality development, understanding personal values and ethics plays a crucial role. This chapter delves into the importance of recognizing and embracing one's values and ethics and how they shape an individual's character and actions. It is essential reading for students, parents, teachers and trainers who are invested in the holistic growth of individuals.

Values are the core beliefs and principles that guide our thoughts, actions and decisions. They act as a moral compass, influencing our behaviour and defining what we consider right or wrong. Personal values differ from person to person, shaped by various factors such as family, culture and personal experiences. By identifying and understanding our values, we gain clarity on what truly matters to us and can align our actions accordingly.

Ethics, on the other hand, refers to the principles and standards of conduct that govern our behaviour in different situations. It is the application of our values in real-life scenarios. Personal ethics serve as a framework for making ethical decisions and engaging in ethical behaviour. By developing a strong ethical foundation, students can navigate through complex situations with integrity and make choices that align with their values.

Recognizing personal values and ethics provides a sense of purpose and direction in life. It helps students understand themselves better and make choices that align with their authentic selves. When students are aware of their values, they can make informed decisions, set meaningful goals and build relationships based on shared values.

This chapter also emphasizes the importance of teachers and parents in nurturing and guiding students on their journey of discovering personal values and ethics. Teachers and trainers can create a supportive environment that encourages students to reflect on their values and understand the impact of their choices. Parents can engage in open conversations with their children, helping them navigate moral dilemmas and reinforcing ethical behaviour.

By understanding personal values and ethics, students can become responsible citizens who make positive contributions to society. This chapter prompts readers to reflect on their values, contemplate ethical dilemmas and develop a strong ethical compass. It provides practical exercises and real-life examples to deepen the understanding of personal values and ethics, making it an invaluable resource for anyone interested in personality development for students.

Overall, "Understanding Personal Values and Ethics" is a chapter that sheds light on the significance of aligning one's actions with their core values and developing a strong ethical foundation. It serves as a guiding compass for students, parents, teachers and trainers, fostering personal growth and character development in the realm of personality development.

Developing a Strong Moral Compass

In today's fast-paced and ever-changing world, it is crucial for students to develop a strong moral compass. A moral compass serves as a guide, helping individuals make decisions that are ethical, principled and in alignment with their values. In this chapter, we will delve into the importance of developing a moral compass and provide practical tips for students, parents, teachers and trainers to nurture this essential aspect of personality development.

For students, having a strong moral compass is vital for personal growth and success. It helps them navigate through the challenges they face on a daily basis, enabling them to make choices that reflect integrity and empathy. By developing a moral compass, students learn to take responsibility for their actions and understand the impact they have on others. This not only fosters positive relationships but also contributes to a peaceful and harmonious society.

Parents play a crucial role in the development of their child's moral compass. By setting a good example and fostering open communication, parents can instill values such as honesty, respect and compassion in their children. Engaging in conversations about ethical dilemmas and encouraging critical thinking can help students develop a deeper understanding of right and wrong.

Teachers and trainers also have an important role to play in shaping students' moral compass. By incorporating moral education into the curriculum, educators can provide students with opportunities to reflect on their values and explore ethical issues. Encouraging students to engage in community service and acts of kindness further reinforces the importance of empathy and social responsibility.

To develop a strong moral compass, students, parents, teachers and trainers can adopt several strategies. Firstly, practising self-reflection and questioning one's motives and actions can lead to a deeper understanding of one's values. Secondly, fostering empathy and understanding of others' perspectives helps students make ethical decisions that benefit everyone involved. Lastly, encouraging open dialogue and ethical discussions creates a safe space for students to voice their opinions and learn from one another.

In conclusion, developing a strong moral compass is an essential aspect of personality development for students. It not only shapes their character but also equips them with the tools to navigate through life's challenges with integrity and empathy. By fostering open communication, setting a good example and engaging in ethical discussions, students can build a solid foundation for a lifetime of ethical decision-making.

Making Ethical Decisions in Daily Life

In our journey of personality development, one crucial aspect that deserves special attention is making ethical decisions in our daily lives. Ethics provides us with a moral compass, guiding us towards actions that are morally right and just. It helps us navigate through complex situations, ensuring that our choices align with our values and principles. This chapter aims to highlight the importance of ethical decision-making and provide practical strategies to implement in our lives.

As students, parents, teachers and trainers, we encounter various situations that require us to make ethical decisions. Whether it is handling academic dishonesty, dealing with conflicts or facing moral dilemmas, understanding how to make ethical choices is paramount.

The foundation of ethical decision-making lies in self-awareness. We must first reflect upon our values, beliefs and personal code of conduct. This introspection helps us establish a strong ethical framework that serves as a guide for our actions.

One essential aspect of ethical decision-making is considering the potential consequences of our choices. We must assess the impact our decisions will have on ourselves and others, ensuring that they promote fairness, respect and empathy. By putting ourselves in the shoes of those affected by our decisions, we can make more informed and ethical choices.

Another crucial element is seeking guidance from trusted individuals or mentors who can provide valuable insights and advice. Engaging in open and honest conversations allows us to gain different perspectives, broadening our understanding of ethical dilemmas and potential solutions.

Furthermore, ethical decision-making involves being accountable for our actions. It requires us to take responsibility for the choices we make and the impact they have on ourselves and others. By holding ourselves to high ethical standards, we contribute to a culture of integrity and promote ethical behaviour in our communities.

In daily life, ethical decisions often require us to make sacrifices or choose the harder path. It is important to understand that making ethical choices may not always be easy, but it is always worth it. By consistently practising ethical decision-making, we build a strong foundation of integrity, resilience and character.

In conclusion, making ethical decisions in our daily lives is a vital aspect of personality development. It requires self-awareness, consideration of consequences, seeking guidance and being accountable for our actions. As students, parents, teachers and trainers embracing ethical decision-making empowers us to create a positive impact in our personal and professional lives, fostering a culture of integrity and ethical behaviour.

Key Takeaways:

- Personal values guide decisions and shape character.
- Strong ethics foster trustworthiness and respect.

Call to Action Exercises:

For Students:

1. **Values List**: Write down five values that matter to you.

   i)

   ii)

   iii)

   iv)

   v)

2. **Decision Reflection**: Think of a recent decision you made and how your values influenced it.

3. **Integrity Challenge**: Commit to one action that aligns with your values each day.

For Parents:

1. **Discuss Values**: Share family values and discuss how they shape behaviour.
2. **Model Integrity**: Show honesty and respect in your daily actions.
3. **Encourage Ethical Choices**: Encourage your child to make decisions that reflect their values.

For Teachers/Trainers:

1. **Values Exercise**: Have students reflect on their values and how these affect their choices.
2. **Ethics Debate**: Organize a debate on ethical issues to encourage critical thinking.
3. **Class Code of Ethics**: Create a set of ethical guidelines together as a class.

Chapter 11 Embracing Diversity and Cultivating Empathy

Appreciating and Embracing Diversity

Appreciating and Embracing Diversity: Celebrating the Beauty of Differences

In today's rapidly changing world, diversity has become an ever-present aspect of our lives. Whether it's the people we interact with, the cultures we encounter or the ideas we exchange, diversity is all around us. It is crucial for students, parents, teachers and trainers to recognize and appreciate the value of diversity in order to build strong foundations for personality development. In this chapter, we will explore the importance of embracing diversity and how it can positively impact our lives.

Understanding Diversity:

Diversity encompasses a wide range of differences, including but not limited to race, ethnicity, gender, religion, socio-economic status, abilities and sexual orientation. Each person's uniqueness adds richness and depth to our society. By acknowledging and respecting these differences, we can foster an environment of inclusivity and acceptance.

Benefits of Embracing Diversity:

Appreciating diversity has numerous benefits, both personally and professionally. Firstly, it broadens our horizons and exposes us to new perspectives, ideas and cultures. By embracing diversity, we become more open-minded and adaptable, enhancing our ability to navigate the complexities of the world. Additionally, diverse teams and communities are known to be more creative, innovative and resilient, as various perspectives and experiences contribute to well-rounded decision-making and problem-solving.

Promoting Inclusivity:

In order to embrace diversity, we must actively promote inclusivity. This means creating safe spaces where everyone feels valued, respected and heard. Students, parents, teachers and trainers all play a significant role in fostering inclusivity within educational institutions. Encouraging open dialogue, teaching empathy and challenging stereotypes are some ways to promote inclusivity and create a harmonious environment.

Celebrating Differences:

One of the most powerful ways to appreciate diversity is by celebrating differences. Through cultural events, festivals and discussions, students can learn about various traditions, customs and beliefs. This not only fosters a sense of pride in one's own culture but also encourages curiosity and understanding of others. By recognizing and celebrating the beauty of our differences, we can break down barriers and build bridges of unity.

Conclusion:

Appreciating and embracing diversity is not only the foundation of personality development but also essential for creating a just and harmonious society. By understanding the importance of diversity, promoting inclusivity and celebrating differences, students, parents, teachers and trainers can collectively contribute to a world that values and respects every individual. Let us embark on this journey of appreciation and embrace the diversity that surrounds us, for it is through diversity that we can truly build strong foundations for personality development.

Developing Cultural Sensitivity and Inclusivity

In today's diverse world, it is crucial for students to develop cultural sensitivity and inclusivity. This chapter aims to provide students, parents, teachers and trainers with valuable insights and strategies to foster an inclusive mindset and embrace cultural diversity. By understanding and appreciating different cultures, students can cultivate a strong foundation for their personality development.

Cultural sensitivity is the ability to recognize and respect the values, beliefs and customs of individuals from different cultural backgrounds. It involves being open-minded and avoiding stereotypes or biases. Inclusivity, on the other hand, refers to creating an environment where everyone feels valued, respected and included regardless of their cultural, ethnic or social background.

To develop cultural sensitivity, students must first acknowledge their own cultural biases and assumptions. They should be encouraged to question their beliefs and be open to learning about other cultures. This can be achieved through various activities such as attending cultural events, interacting with diverse groups and reading literature from different parts of the world.

Parents play a vital role in shaping their child's cultural sensitivity. By exposing children to different cultures from an early age, parents can instill a sense of curiosity and respect for diversity. They can organize family trips to culturally significant places, encourage their children to make friends from different backgrounds and engage in discussions about cultural differences and similarities.

Teachers and trainers also have a responsibility to promote inclusivity and cultural sensitivity in the classroom. They can incorporate diverse perspectives and multicultural resources in their lessons. By creating a safe and inclusive space for students to share their cultural experiences, teachers can foster empathy, understanding and respect among students. Additionally, teachers can encourage collaborative learning activities that bring together students from various backgrounds, promoting teamwork and cross-cultural understanding.

In conclusion, developing cultural sensitivity and inclusivity is essential for students' personality development. By embracing diversity and understanding different cultures, students become more empathetic, adaptable and open-minded individuals. With the support of parents, teachers and trainers, students can build strong foundations for their personal growth and contribute to creating a harmonious and inclusive society.

Cultivating Empathy towards Others

Empathy is a powerful tool that helps us understand and connect with others on a deeper level. It is the ability to put oneself in someone else's shoes, to see the world from their perspective and to truly understand their emotions, thoughts and experiences. In the fast-paced and often self-centred world we live in, empathy is a skill that needs to be nurtured and developed. In this chapter, we will explore the importance of cultivating empathy towards others and how it can contribute to a student's overall personality development.

For Students:

Developing empathy is not only beneficial for your personal growth but also for your academic success. By understanding others' perspectives, you can enhance your communication skills, resolve conflicts effectively and build healthier relationships. Empathy enables you to be more compassionate, patient and kind, qualities that can make you a well-rounded individual. In this chapter, you will learn practical strategies to cultivate empathy, such as active listening, asking open-ended questions and practising empathy in everyday situations.

1. Understanding the Power of Empathy:

Empathy, in its essence, is the ability to understand and share the feelings of others. It goes beyond sympathy, requiring an emotional connection that allows you to step into someone else's shoes. For students, recognizing the power of empathy is crucial for personal growth. It not only enhances your emotional intelligence but also contributes significantly to academic success. By grasping others' perspectives, you gain a more profound understanding of various subjects and improve your problem-solving skills.

Empathy is a transformative skill that fosters a sense of connection with fellow students, teachers and the broader community. It creates an environment where collaboration thrives, enabling you to work effectively in group settings. This section will delve into the psychological and academic benefits of empathy, demonstrating how it can positively shape your journey through education.

2. Practical Strategies for Cultivating Empathy:

Cultivating empathy involves adopting practical strategies that can be applied in everyday situations. Active listening is a cornerstone of empathetic communication. It requires not just hearing but truly understanding the emotions and thoughts behind the words. Open-ended questions facilitate meaningful conversations, allowing you to explore others' perspectives more deeply. Through real-life scenarios and role-playing exercises, you'll have the opportunity to put these strategies into practice.

Furthermore, empathy extends beyond the academic realm, influencing your interactions with friends, family and the broader community. By honing these practical skills, you develop a well-rounded approach to empathy, making it an integral part of your personal and academic life.

3. Building Healthy Relationships:

Empathy forms the base of healthy relationships. Understanding others' emotions creates a strong foundation for meaningful connections. This section will explore how empathy contributes to the development of trust, compassion and effective communication in relationships. It will also address the role of empathy in conflict resolution, emphasizing its power to de-escalate tense situations and build bridges between differing perspectives.

As you delve into the importance of empathy in building healthy relationships, you'll gain insights into how it enhances teamwork and cooperation. Real-life examples will showcase how empathy can transform conflicts into opportunities for growth, fostering an environment where everyone feels heard and understood.

4. Compassion, Patience and Kindness:

Compassion, patience and kindness are virtues that are closely intertwined with empathy. This section will explore how empathy serves as the foundation for cultivating these qualities. By understanding, you develop a genuine sense of compassion for their struggles. This, in turn, leads to increased patience and a kinder approach in your interactions.

Real-life examples and case studies will illustrate how individuals who practice empathy exhibit greater compassion and kindness in various life situations. Through these stories, you'll gain a deeper understanding of how empathy can be a driving force behind creating a positive and supportive community.

For Parents:

As parents, it is crucial to teach your children the value of empathy from an early age. Empathy helps children develop emotional intelligence, which is essential for their overall well-being. By fostering empathy, you can raise children who are compassionate, understanding and respectful towards others. This chapter will provide you with tips and activities to encourage empathy in your child, such as modeling empathy, encouraging perspective-taking and practising gratitude.

1. Teaching Empathy from Early Childhood:

Implanting empathy in children starts from an early age. This section will explore the importance of introducing empathy to children during their formative years. Parents can provide insights into the cognitive and emotional development of empathy in children and highlight the pivotal role parents play in this process.

Practical tips and age-appropriate activities will be shared to guide parents in fostering empathy. By understanding the unique challenges and opportunities presented at different developmental stages, parents can create a nurturing environment that encourages the growth of empathetic behaviour.

2. Fostering Emotional Intelligence:

Emotional intelligence is a key component of a child's overall well-being. This section will explore how empathy contributes to the development of emotional intelligence in children. It is important to highlight the interconnectedness of empathy, self-awareness and social skills, emphasizing the life-long benefits of nurturing emotional intelligence from a young age.

Through engaging activities and scenarios, parents will gain practical strategies to foster emotional intelligence in their children. By weaving empathy into daily interactions and encouraging open communication, parents can create a supportive environment that nurtures their child's emotional growth.

3. Modeling Empathy as a Parent:

Parents serve as primary role models for their children. This section will emphasize the importance of modeling empathy in daily interactions. Parents can provide guidance and demonstrate empathetic behaviour through active listening, understanding non-verbal cues and healthily expressing emotions.

Real-life stories and case studies will illustrate the profound impact of parental empathy on a child's character development. By embodying empathy, parents not only teach the value of understanding others but also lay the foundation for a compassionate and considerate worldview in their children.

4. Encouraging Perspective-Taking and Gratitude:

Perspective-taking is a skill that enhances empathy by enabling children to see situations from different viewpoints. This section will explore the role of perspective-taking in developing empathy and provide parents with practical activities to encourage this skill in their children.

Additionally, the section will delve into the connection between empathy and gratitude. By fostering a sense of gratitude, parents can instill in their children an appreciation for the perspectives and experiences of others. Activities and exercises will be helpful to parents to incorporate these practices into their family routines, creating a home environment that nurtures empathy.

For Teachers and Trainers:

Empathy plays a significant role in creating a positive and inclusive learning environment. By cultivating empathy in your students, you can promote a sense of belonging, reduce bullying and enhance overall classroom dynamics. This chapter will offer you strategies to incorporate empathy-building activities in your teaching, such as group discussions, role-playing exercises and reflective writing assignments. You will also gain insights into how to model empathy as an educator and create opportunities for students to practice empathy inside and outside the classroom.

1. The Role of Empathy in Learning Environments:

A positive and inclusive learning environment is essential for academic success. This section will explore how empathy plays a pivotal role in creating such an atmosphere. It will delve into the correlation between empathy and a sense of belonging, as well as the impact of empathy on reducing bullying and fostering positive classroom dynamics.

Practical insights and research-backed strategies will be shared to help teachers understand how empathy contributes to the overall well-being and academic achievements of their students. By recognizing the importance of empathy, educators can create a learning space that promotes collaboration, respect and understanding.

2. Incorporating Empathy-Building Activities:

Engaging students in empathy-building activities is a powerful way to instill this skill. Teachers and trainers can provide a range of activities, from group discussions to role-playing exercises, designed to enhance empathy among students. These activities can be seamlessly integrated into various subjects and extracurricular programs.

Case studies and success stories will showcase the positive outcomes of incorporating empathy-building activities in educational settings. By implementing these strategies, teachers can create a dynamic and empathetic classroom environment that empowers students to prosper both academically and personally.

3. Modeling Empathy as an Educator:

Educators serve as mentors and guides for their students. This section will delve into strategies for teachers to model empathy in their teaching methods. They can highlight the importance of creating a supportive and empathetic teacher-student relationship, emphasizing the impact of such relationships on students' overall learning experiences.

Real-life examples and testimonials from educators who have successfully integrated empathy into their teaching practices can be shared. By modeling empathy, teachers inspire students to adopt empathetic behaviours, creating a positive ripple effect throughout the entire learning community.

4. Creating Opportunities for Empathy Practice:

Empathy, like any skill, requires practice. This section will provide teachers and trainers with practical ways to create opportunities for students to practice and reinforce empathy. From reflective writing assignments to community service projects, these activities will encourage students to apply empathetic principles in real-life situations.

By fostering empathy towards others, students can develop strong interpersonal skills, build meaningful relationships and contribute to a more empathetic and compassionate society. This chapter will equip students, parents, teachers and trainers with the necessary tools and knowledge to cultivate empathy, making it an integral part of their personality development journey. Let us embark on this path of empathy together and create a world where compassion and understanding are the foundations of our interactions.

Key Takeaways:

- Embracing diversity promotes understanding and acceptance of others.
- Empathy fosters deeper connections and enhances emotional intelligence.

Call to Action Exercises:

For Students:

1. **Diverse Friendships**: Make a friend from a different background and learn about their culture.
2. **Empathy Journal**: Write about a time you felt misunderstood and how it felt.
3. **Kindness Challenge**: Perform one kind act daily for someone outside your close circle.

For Parents:

1. **Discuss Diversity**: Talk about different cultures and the importance of empathy.
2. **Model Inclusion**: Show acceptance and respect toward people from diverse backgrounds.

3. **Family Kindness Project**: Choose a group to volunteer with to support those in need.

For Teachers/Trainers:

1. **Cultural Awareness Activity**: Introduce students to a new culture each week.
2. **Empathy Reflection**: Encourage students to reflect on how empathy affects relationships.
3. **Group Projects**: Assign group projects to help students work with peers from different backgrounds.

Chapter 12 Continuous Self-Improvement and Life-Long Learning

The Importance of Life-Long Learning

In today's world, the importance of life-long learning cannot be emphasized enough. As students, parents, teachers and trainers, we all play a crucial role in shaping the personality development of students. Life-long learning is a key component of this process, as it empowers individuals to adapt, grow and succeed in an ever-evolving society.

Life-long learning goes beyond the traditional classroom setting. It encompasses a mindset that fosters continuous personal and professional growth. It involves seeking knowledge, acquiring new skills and developing a curious and open-minded approach to life. By embracing life-long learning, students can enhance their academic performance, broaden their horizons and become mature individuals.

For students, life-long learning equips them with the tools and skills needed to navigate the challenges of today's world. It encourages critical thinking, problem-solving and innovation, which enables them to thrive in a competitive job market. Moreover, it instills a sense of self-confidence and resilience, empowering students to overcome obstacles and achieve their goals.

Parents play a vital role in fostering a culture of life-long learning. By encouraging their children to explore new interests, pursue hobbies and engage in extracurricular activities, parents can cultivate a love for learning that extends beyond the classroom. They can provide support and guidance, helping their children discover their passions and nurturing their intellectual curiosity.

Teachers and trainers have a unique opportunity to inspire and guide students on their life-long learning journey. By creating interactive and engaging learning environments, they can foster a love for learning that extends far beyond grades or exams. They can encourage students to ask questions, think critically and pursue knowledge independently. By embracing innovative teaching methods and incorporating real-world examples, teachers and trainers can make learning meaningful and relevant.

In today's fast-paced world, where technology and information are constantly evolving, life-long learning is no longer an option; it is a necessity. The ability to adapt, learn and grow throughout our lives is crucial for personal and professional success. By embracing life-long learning, students can build strong foundations for their future, parents can nurture their children's intellectual growth and teachers and trainers can inspire a generation of life-long learners.

So, let us commit to life-long learning, for it is through continuous education that we can unlock our true potential and create a better tomorrow.

Strategies for Continuous Self-Improvement

In today's competitive world, it is essential for students to continuously work on their personal growth and development. Building strong foundations in personality development is crucial to thrive in various aspects of life. This chapter aims to provide valuable strategies that will empower students to embark on a journey of continuous self-improvement.

1. Set Clear Goals: Begin by setting clear and achievable goals that align with your aspirations and values. By defining what you want to accomplish, whether it's academic, personal or professional, you create a roadmap for your self-improvement journey.

2. Embrace Life-long Learning: Cultivate a thirst for knowledge and seek opportunities to learn beyond the classroom. Engage in reading books, attending workshops or enrolling in online courses. Continuously expanding your knowledge base will enhance your skills and keep you ahead of the curve.

3. Develop Self-Awareness: Understand your strengths, weaknesses and preferences. Self-awareness allows you to identify areas for improvement and capitalize on your strengths. Reflect on your actions, seek feedback from mentors and adjust your approach accordingly.

4. Practice Self-Discipline: Develop the habit of self-discipline to stay focused and committed to your goals. Set routines, prioritize tasks and eliminate distractions to optimize your productivity.

5. Embrace Failure as a Learning Opportunity: Rather than fearing failure, view it as an opportunity to learn and grow. Embrace challenges, take risks and use setbacks as stepping stones towards success. Learn from your mistakes, adapt and continue.

6. Cultivate a Growth Mindset: Adopt a growth mindset, believing that your abilities can be developed through dedication and hard work. Embrace challenges, view feedback as constructive and remain resilient in the face of obstacles.

7. Seek Mentorship: Surround yourself with positive role models who inspire and guide you. Seek mentors, whether it's a teacher, parent or industry professional, who can provide valuable insights and support your personal growth.

8. Practice Self-Care: Take care of your physical, mental and emotional well-being. Prioritize sleep, exercise regularly, maintain healthy relationships and practice mindfulness or meditation. Nurturing yourself holistically will enhance your overall development.

9. Foster a Growth-Oriented Environment: Surround yourself with like-minded individuals who are also committed to personal growth. Engage in meaningful discussions, collaborate and support each other's endeavors. Create an environment that fosters growth and positivity.

10. Celebrate Successes: Acknowledge and celebrate your achievements, no matter how small they may seem. Rewarding yourself for reaching milestones will boost your motivation and inspire further self-improvement.

By implementing these strategies for continuous self-improvement, students can build strong foundations in personality development. Remember, personal growth is a life-long journey and by investing in yourself, you equip yourself with the tools necessary to succeed in all aspects of life.

Embracing Challenges and Seeking Growth Opportunities

In the pursuit of personal and academic growth, students need to embrace challenges and actively seek out opportunities for development. This chapter aims to provide valuable insights and guidance on how to foster a mindset of growth and maximize one's potential.

For students, challenges can initially seem daunting and overwhelming. However, it is crucial to understand that challenges are not obstacles but rather stepping stones towards personal growth. By embracing challenges, students can develop resilience, determination and a strong sense of self-belief. It is through overcoming these challenges that they can unlock their true potential and discover their capabilities.

Parents play a vital role in supporting their children's growth by encouraging them to face challenges head-on. By providing a nurturing and supportive environment, parents can instill in their children the belief that they are capable of achieving great things. They can also guide their children in setting realistic goals and help them develop strategies to overcome obstacles along the way.

Teachers and trainers, on the other hand, are responsible for creating a conducive learning environment that encourages students to take on challenges. By designing engaging and enriching activities, educators can help students develop problem-solving skills, critical thinking abilities and a growth mindset. It is important for teachers to provide constructive feedback and celebrate students' efforts, fostering a sense of accomplishment and motivating them to seek further growth opportunities.

To embrace challenges and seek growth opportunities, students need to cultivate a growth mindset. This mindset helps students view challenges as opportunities for learning and growth rather than as failures. By adopting a growth mindset, students develop a love for life-long learning, are open to new experiences and are willing to step out of their comfort zones.

In conclusion, embracing challenges and seeking growth opportunities is crucial for students' personality development. Through a combination of support from parents, guidance from teachers and a growth mindset, students can overcome obstacles, maximize their potential and become well-rounded individuals. By embracing challenges, students will not only grow academically but also develop essential life skills that will prepare them for future success.

Key Takeaways:

- Life-long learning fuels personal and professional growth.
- A commitment to improvement makes us adaptable and resilient.

Call to Action Exercises:

For Students:

1. **Weekly Learning Goal**: Choose a new skill or topic to learn about each week.
2. **Self-Assessment**: Reflect on what you want to improve and make a simple plan.
3. **Skill-Building Activity**: Pick one hobby and dedicate time to improving it.

For Parents:

1. **Support Hobbies**: Encourage your child's interests by providing resources and guidance.
2. **Learning Together**: Take on a new learning challenge as a family.

3. **Share Growth Stories**: Talk about a skill you developed through practice.

For Teachers/Trainers:

1. **Continuous Learning Pledge**: Have students commit to learning something new each month.
2. **Skill Development Week**: Dedicate a week to exploring new skills or topics in class.
3. **Celebrate Progress**: Recognize students' efforts to learn and improve continuously.

Chapter 13: Overcoming Obstacles and Adversities

Dealing with Failure and Setbacks

Failure and setbacks are a natural part of life and they can often be challenging to navigate. However, students must develop the resilience and skills necessary to handle these obstacles effectively. In this chapter, we will explore various strategies for dealing with failure and setbacks, helping students build strong foundations for their personality development.

1. Shifting perspective: Instead of viewing failure as a negative outcome, students need to understand that it is an opportunity for growth and learning. Encourage them to reframe their mindset and see setbacks as valuable lessons that can propel them forward.

2. Self-reflection: After experiencing a failure or setback, students should take the time to reflect on what went wrong and why. This process of self-reflection allows them to gain insights into their strengths and weaknesses, enabling them to make necessary adjustments for future endeavours.

3. Setting realistic goals: Unrealistic or overly ambitious goals can lead to disappointment and setbacks. Teach students the importance of setting realistic and achievable goals, allowing them to experience success and build confidence gradually.

4. Developing resilience: Resilience is a crucial trait for handling failure and setbacks. Students should be taught how to bounce back from disappointments, develop a positive mindset and persevere through challenges. Encourage them to seek support from teachers, parents or mentors during tough times.

5. Embracing failure as a stepping stone: Students need to understand that failure is not the end but a stepping stone towards success. Sharing stories of successful individuals who have faced numerous setbacks can inspire and motivate them to keep going.

6. Encouraging perseverance: Teach students the value of persistence and determination. Help them understand that setbacks are temporary and that success often requires multiple attempts. Encourage them to keep pushing forward, even when the going gets tough.

7. Cultivating a growth mindset: Developing a growth mindset is essential for handling failure and setbacks effectively. Students should be encouraged to believe in their ability to improve and develop their skills through hard work and dedication.

8. Seeking support: Students should be aware that seeking support is not a sign of weakness but a strength. Encourage them to reach out to teachers,

parents or mentors for guidance and support during difficult times.

By equipping students with strategies to deal with failure and setbacks, we can help them develop a strong foundation for their personality development. Remember, it is through overcoming obstacles that we grow and become resilient individuals capable of achieving great success.

Strategies for Overcoming Obstacles

In life, we often encounter obstacles that can hinder our progress and success. These challenges can come in various forms, such as academic difficulties, personal setbacks or even external factors beyond our control. However, it is crucial to understand that overcoming obstacles is an essential part of personal growth and development. In this chapter, we will explore some strategies that can help students overcome obstacles and build strong foundations for their personality development.

1. Embrace a growth mindset: A growth mindset is the belief that our abilities and intelligence can be developed through dedication, hard work and resilience. By adopting this perspective, students can face obstacles as opportunities for growth rather than setbacks. Encourage students to view challenges as stepping stones to success and emphasize the importance of perseverance.

2. Set realistic goals: Setting realistic and achievable goals is crucial when facing obstacles. Teach students to break down larger goals into smaller, manageable tasks. By doing so, they can build momentum and gain a sense of accomplishment, which can ultimately help them overcome obstacles more effectively.

3. Seek support: Encourage students to reach out for support when facing obstacles. This can include seeking help from teachers, parents or trainers who can provide guidance and assistance. Additionally, students can benefit from collaborating with peers who may have faced similar challenges or can offer different perspectives.

4. Develop problem-solving skills: Problem-solving skills are essential for overcoming obstacles. Encourage students to approach challenges systematically by identifying the problem, brainstorming possible solutions and evaluating the pros and cons of each option. By developing these skills, students will become more equipped to overcome obstacles effectively.

5. Cultivate resilience: Resilience is the ability to bounce back from adversity. Teach students that setbacks and obstacles are a natural part of life and it is important to develop resilience to navigate through them successfully. Encourage students to reflect on their strengths and past successes to build

resilience and maintain a positive attitude in the face of challenges.

By implementing these strategies, students can develop a strong foundation for their personality development. Overcoming obstacles not only builds resilience but also fosters self-confidence and adaptability, which are crucial traits for personal growth and success. Remember, it is in the face of challenges that our true potential shines brightest.

Building Resilience in the Face of Adversity

In the journey of life, we often come across challenges and setbacks that test our strength and character. Adversity can come in various forms, such as academic difficulties, personal struggles or even unexpected events like the global pandemic. However, it is important to remember that resilience is the key to overcoming these obstacles and emerging stronger on the other side. In this chapter, we will explore the concept of building resilience in the face of adversity, providing valuable insights and practical strategies for students, parents, teachers and trainers in the field of personality development.

Resilience is not something we are born with, but rather a skill that can be cultivated and nurtured over time. Developing resilience is crucial for students as it equips them with the tools to navigate through life's challenges with confidence and determination. It helps them bounce back from failures, setbacks and disappointments, enabling them to keep moving forward towards their goals.

For students, resilience starts with a growth mindset. Understanding that failures and setbacks are not permanent but rather opportunities for learning and growth is essential. This mindset shift allows students to view challenges as stepping stones towards personal development. Additionally, developing self-awareness and emotional intelligence helps students recognize and manage their emotions effectively, enabling them to cope with adversity healthily and constructively.

Parents, teachers and trainers also play a vital role in fostering resilience in students. By creating a supportive and nurturing environment, they can encourage students to take on challenges and provide them with the necessary guidance and resources to overcome obstacles. Teaching problem-solving skills, promoting positive self-talk and fostering a sense of belonging within the student community are all effective strategies for building resilience.

In this chapter, we will delve into various practical exercises and techniques that can be implemented to build resilience. From mindfulness practices that promote self-reflection and stress reduction to goal-setting strategies that encourage perseverance, students, parents, teachers and trainers will find a wealth of tools to enhance their resilience skills.

Below is a detailed exploration of the practices and techniques required for building resilience:

For Students:

1. Mindfulness Practices for Self-Reflection:

Mindfulness involves being fully present and engaged in the current moment. To build resilience, students can start with simple mindfulness practices. Encourage them to find a quiet space, sit comfortably and focus on their breath. Guided mindfulness exercises, available through Apps or online resources, can aid in cultivating self-awareness and reflection. By regularly practising mindfulness, students develop the ability to stay calm in challenging situations and gain a deeper understanding of their emotions.

2. Stress Reduction Techniques:

Identifying stressors is the first step in managing them effectively. Students can create a stress journal to pinpoint sources of stress. Techniques such as deep breathing exercises, progressive muscle relaxation and guided imagery can be incorporated into their daily routines. These practices help to activate the body's relaxation response, reducing stress hormones and promoting a sense of calm. Encouraging students to adopt stress reduction as a proactive habit fosters long-term resilience.

3. Goal-Setting for Perseverance:

Setting goals is a powerful strategy for building resilience. Guide students in setting realistic and achievable short-term and long-term goals. Break larger goals into smaller, manageable tasks. Regular reflection on progress, celebrating small victories and adjusting goals as needed help instill perseverance. The process of working towards and achieving goals builds resilience by teaching students that setbacks are part of the journey and that adaptability is crucial for success.

4. Building a Positive Mindset:

Resilience is closely tied to having a positive mindset. Students can cultivate optimism and gratitude through daily practices. Encourage them to keep a gratitude journal, reflecting on the positive aspects of their day. Introduce activities that challenge negative thought patterns and promote positive self-talk. Fostering a positive mindset helps students view challenges as opportunities for growth, reinforcing their ability to bounce back from adversity.

For Parents:

1. Nurturing Mindfulness in Children:

Introducing mindfulness to children involves age-appropriate activities. For younger children, activities like mindful colouring or listening to calming music can be effective. Older children may benefit from short guided mindfulness sessions. Parents can create a mindful home environment by modeling mindfulness practices and establishing tech-free zones during meals or before bedtime. Recognizing and addressing stressors in a child's life promotes open communication and provides opportunities for parental support.

2. Family Stress Reduction Strategies:

Identifying family stressors is crucial for creating a harmonious home environment. Family-friendly stress reduction exercises, such as family walks or relaxation sessions, can be implemented. Establishing regular family meetings to discuss stressors and collaboratively finding solutions fosters open communication. Creating a supportive atmosphere where family members feel comfortable expressing their concerns contributes to a resilient family dynamic.

3. Instilling Resilience through Encouragement:

Parents play a crucial role in instilling resilience through encouragement. Communicate the value of effort and perseverance over immediate success. Praise children for their resilience in the face of challenges, emphasizing the process rather than just the outcome. Provide constructive feedback that focuses on effort, strategy and improvement. Encouraging a growth mindset, where challenges are seen as opportunities to learn, builds resilience in children.

4. Modeling Resilience as a Parent:

Parents can model resilience through personal examples. Share stories of overcoming challenges and setbacks, highlighting the lessons learned. Expressing emotions openly and demonstrating healthy coping mechanisms reinforces that resilience involves acknowledging and adapting to difficulties. Encourage children to view failures as opportunities for growth, emphasizing that setbacks are a natural part of life's journey.

For Teachers and Trainers:

1. Integrating Mindfulness in the Classroom:

Teachers can integrate mindfulness into the classroom by starting with short, simple exercises. Begin each class with a brief mindfulness practice, such as a mindful breathing exercise or a moment of silence. Create a supportive environment by establishing clear expectations for respect and understanding. Address potential challenges by fostering a culture of openness, where students feel comfortable discussing their experiences with mindfulness.

2. Classroom Stress Reduction Techniques:

Identifying academic stressors is essential for implementing stress reduction techniques. Teachers can introduce short stress-reduction activities during class, such as quick relaxation exercises or mindfulness breaks. Collaborative approaches, such as group discussions on managing stress, create a sense of shared responsibility for the class community's well-being. By acknowledging and addressing stressors collectively, teachers contribute to a resilient and supportive classroom culture.

3. Goal-Setting Workshops for Students:

Organizing goal-setting workshops involves providing students with tools and resources for effective goal-setting.

Teachers can guide students through the process of setting SMART goals (Specific, Measurable, Achievable, Relevant, Time-bound). Facilitate discussions on the importance of persistence and adaptability in achieving goals. Encourage students to reflect on their progress regularly and make adjustments as needed, fostering a mindset of continuous improvement.

4. Promoting Resilience through Classroom Culture:

Establishing a positive and supportive classroom culture is foundational for promoting resilience. Teachers can create an environment where students feel valued and supported by incorporating collaborative learning activities. Encourage peer support and collaboration, emphasizing the importance of helping each other navigate challenges. Integrate resilience-building concepts into the curriculum, connecting academic learning with real-life skills that promote adaptability and perseverance.

For all (in General – for Students, Parents, Teachers and Trainers):

1. Collaborative Resilience-Building Activities:

Engaging in group activities that involve students, parents, teachers and trainers fosters a sense of community resilience. Activities could include team-building exercises, workshops or projects that promote mutual support and understanding. Creating opportunities for cross-generational learning enhances the richness of the resilience-building experience.

2. Reflective Journaling for Personal Growth:

Introducing reflective journaling as a tool for personal growth involves providing prompts and guidance. Encourage individuals to regularly journal about their challenges, successes and lessons learned. Reflective journaling promotes self-awareness and allows individuals to track their resilience-building journey. Emphasize the value of regular self-reflection as a cornerstone of personal development.

3. Community Workshops on Resilience:

Organizing community workshops on resilience involves creating a space for shared learning and support. Invite guest speakers to share personal stories of resilience, providing inspiration and practical insights. Facilitate networking opportunities for individuals to connect, share experiences and learn from one another. Community workshops contribute to building a resilient and interconnected support network.

4. Resilience-Building Challenges and Initiatives:

Launching resilience-building challenges involves setting achievable goals for individuals and groups. Challenges could include tasks that promote adaptability, perseverance and collaboration. Engage in community initiatives that address specific resilience-related themes, fostering a collective commitment to building a resilient community. Celebrate and acknowledge milestones achieved, reinforcing the importance of ongoing resilience efforts.

Building Strong Foundations: Personality Development for Students aims to equip individuals with the necessary skills and mindset to thrive in an ever-changing world. By embracing resilience and learning how to face adversity head-on, students can build a solid foundation for personal growth and success. This chapter will serve as a valuable resource for anyone seeking to enhance their resilience skills and navigate through life's challenges with determination, courage and resilience.

Key Takeaways:

- Challenges are an inevitable part of life and provide growth opportunities.
- Developing resilience and problem-solving skills helps in tackling obstacles effectively.

Call to Action Exercises:

For Students:

1. **Challenge Journal**: Write about a recent challenge and the steps you took to handle it.
2. **Problem-Solving Practice**: Pick a small issue in your life and brainstorm three ways to address it.
3. **Positive Reframing**: List three "lessons learned" from past setbacks and what they taught you.

For Parents:

1. **Encourage Perseverance**: Share a story of a challenge you faced and how you overcame it.
2. **Reframe Setbacks**: Help your child see failures as learning experiences, not just losses.

3. **Celebrate Small Wins**: Recognize even small steps your child takes to overcome their difficulties.

For Teachers/Trainers:

1. **Resilience Workshop**: Organize activities focused on resilience.
2. **Classroom Encouragement**: Share examples of people who faced adversity and succeeded.
3. **Guided Reflection**: Help students reflect on how they can grow from challenges.

Chapter 14
Creating a Positive Mindset

The Power of a Positive Mindset

In this chapter, we delve into the remarkable potential of cultivating a positive mindset and how it can profoundly impact the personality development of students. A positive mindset encompasses an optimistic and proactive approach towards challenges, setbacks and even everyday situations. It involves a conscious choice to focus on the good, embrace growth and maintain a can-do attitude.

For students, a positive mindset can be a game-changer. It not only influences their academic performance but also shapes their overall well-being and success in life. The power of a positive mindset lies in its ability to foster resilience, enhance problem-solving skills and boost self-confidence.

When faced with difficulties, a positive mindset helps students see obstacles as opportunities for growth and learning. Instead of being discouraged by failures, they view them as stepping stones towards improvement. By reframing setbacks in this way, students become more resilient and develop the ability to bounce back .stronger than before.

Moreover, a positive mindset empowers students to approach problem-solving with creativity and innovation. It allows them to think out of the box, explore diverse solutions and continue until they find the best possible outcome. This mindset shift opens doors to new possibilities and fosters a sense of resourcefulness within students.

Alongside resilience and problem-solving skills, a positive mindset also plays a crucial role in building self-confidence. Students who believe in their abilities and maintain a positive outlook are more likely to take on challenges with enthusiasm and embrace new opportunities. This confidence acts as a catalyst for personal growth, enabling students to step out of their comfort zones and explore their full potential.

Parents, teachers and trainers also have a vital role to play in nurturing a positive mindset among students. By providing encouragement, constructive feedback and creating an environment that fosters positivity, they can help students develop a strong foundation for personality development.

In conclusion, the power of a positive mindset should not be underestimated. It has the potential to transform the lives of students, enhancing their resilience, problem-solving skills and self-confidence. By cultivating a positive mindset, students can overcome challenges, seize opportunities and grow into well-rounded individuals. Parents, teachers and trainers have a crucial role in fostering a positive mindset among students and setting them on a path of life-long success.

Techniques for Cultivating a Positive Mindset

In today's fast-paced and demanding world, cultivating a positive mindset is crucial for students' personal and academic success. A positive mindset helps in building resilience, reducing stress and fostering well-being. This chapter explores effective techniques for cultivating a positive mindset, empowering students to develop strong foundations in personality development.

1. Practice Gratitude: Encouraging students to practice gratitude is a powerful technique to shift their focus from negativity to positivity. Regularly expressing gratitude for the things they have, the people in their lives and their achievements helps students develop a more optimistic outlook.

2. Positive Affirmations: The use of positive affirmations can rewire students' thought patterns and replace negative self-talk with empowering beliefs. Encourage students to create personalized affirmations that align with their goals and values. Regularly repeating these affirmations helps to reprogram their subconscious mind.

3. Embrace Failure as a Learning Opportunity: Students should be taught to view failure as a stepping stone to success rather than a setback. By reframing failure as a learning opportunity, they can develop resilience and grow from their experiences.

4. Surround Yourself with Positivity: The environment we surround ourselves with greatly influences our mindset. Encourage students to connect with positive-minded individuals, whether it be friends, mentors or teachers. Additionally, immersing themselves in uplifting content

such as books, podcasts or motivational videos can inspire and motivate them.

5. Practice Mindfulness and Meditation: Mindfulness and meditation techniques help students develop self-awareness and focus on the present moment. Regular practice of mindfulness exercises enables students to better manage stress, improve concentration and cultivate a positive mindset.

6. Set Realistic Goals: Setting realistic, achievable goals is essential for maintaining a positive mindset. Encourage students to break down their goals into smaller, manageable tasks. Celebrating small wins along the way helps students stay motivated and fosters a sense of achievement.

7. Develop a Growth Mindset: Teach students about the power of a growth mindset, emphasizing that intelligence and abilities can be developed through effort and hard work. Encourage students to embrace challenges, persist in the face of setbacks and see failures as opportunities for growth.

By incorporating these techniques into their daily lives, students can cultivate a positive mindset and lay the foundation for their overall personality development. Parents, teachers and trainers need to support and guide students in practising these techniques, as they play a vital role in shaping the mindset of the next generation.

Overcoming Negative Thinking Patterns

Introduction:

In the journey of personality development, one of the most crucial aspects is learning how to overcome negative thinking patterns. Negative thoughts can hinder personal growth, affect relationships and create obstacles to achieving success. This chapter will provide valuable insights and strategies to help students overcome these detrimental patterns and build a strong foundation for their personality development.

Understanding Negative Thinking Patterns:

Negative thinking patterns often arise from self-doubt, fear of failure or past experiences. These patterns can manifest as self-criticism, pessimism and the tendency to focus on the negatives. Recognizing these patterns is the first step towards overcoming them.

Challenging Negative Thoughts:

To overcome negative thinking patterns, students must challenge their negative thoughts. They can start by questioning the validity of their negative beliefs and evaluating evidence that supports or contradicts them. By replacing negative thoughts with more positive and realistic ones, students can gradually reshape their thinking patterns.

Developing a Growth Mindset:

Adopting a growth mindset is essential for personal development. Students should understand that abilities and intelligence can be developed through dedication and effort. Encouraging a belief in personal growth helps students embrace challenges, learn from failures and maintain a positive outlook.

Practising Self-Compassion:

Self-compassion plays a vital role in overcoming negative thinking patterns. Students should learn to treat themselves with kindness and understanding, just as they would treat a close friend. By acknowledging their strengths and accepting their flaws, students can develop a healthier self-image and overcome self-critical thoughts.

Building a Supportive Network:

Surrounding oneself with positive and supportive individuals can significantly impact personal development. Students should seek out friends, parents, teachers and trainers who uplift and motivate them. Sharing experiences, seeking guidance and receiving constructive feedback from this network can help students overcome negative thinking patterns.

Cultivating Positive Habits:

Engaging in activities that promote positivity can help students break free from negative thinking patterns.

Regular exercise, mindfulness practices and pursuing hobbies can boost confidence, reduce stress and improve overall well-being. By incorporating these habits into their daily routine, students can cultivate a positive mindset and overcome negative thoughts.

Conclusion:

Overcoming negative thinking patterns is a transformative process that requires self-awareness, perseverance and a growth mindset. By challenging negative thoughts, practising self-compassion and cultivating positive habits, students can break free from the shackles of negativity and build a strong foundation for their personality development. Embracing these strategies will not only enhance their personal growth but also positively impact their relationships, academic performance and overall success.

Key Takeaways:

- A positive mindset enhances mental well-being and helps achieve goals.
- Optimism and self-belief are crucial for overcoming negativity and setbacks.

Call to Action Exercises:

For Students:

1. **Daily Affirmations**: Start each day with three positive affirmations about yourself.
2. **Gratitude Practice**: Write down three things you're grateful for each night before bed.
3. **Flip the Negative**: When you think negatively, try to reframe it positively.

For Parents:

1. **Model Positivity**: Demonstrate a positive attitude, especially during stressful times.
2. **Celebrate Positives**: Help your child recognize their accomplishments, no matter how small.

3. **Daily Gratitude Sharing**: Share one thing each day that made you feel grateful.

For Teachers/Trainers:

1. **Positivity Exercise**: Have students write positive affirmations or goals on paper and keep them visible.
2. **Classroom Gratitude Circle**: Each student shares something positive about their day.
3. **Negative Reframing Activity**: Discuss ways to turn negative thoughts into positive ones.

Chapter 15
Personal Branding and Professional Development

The Importance of Personal Branding for Students

In today's increasingly competitive world, personal branding has become more critical than ever before, even for students. It is no longer enough to simply excel academically; students must also focus on building a strong personal brand to stand out from the crowd and achieve their goals. This chapter explores the significance of personal branding for students, providing valuable insights for students, parents, teachers and trainers alike.

Personal branding encompasses the unique qualities, skills and values that individuals possess. By developing a personal brand, students can distinguish themselves from their peers, attract opportunities and create a positive impression on others. It goes beyond academic achievements and focuses on the development of soft skills, interpersonal relationships and self-awareness.

For students, personal branding can unlock a world of opportunities. It helps them discover their strengths and passions, enabling them to make informed choices about their academic and career paths. By understanding their personal brand, students can align their goals and actions with their authentic selves, leading to increased satisfaction and success.

Parents play a crucial role in supporting their children's personal branding journey. By encouraging self-reflection and providing guidance, parents can help students identify their unique qualities and develop strategies for showcasing them effectively. Parents must also emphasize the importance of integrity and authenticity in personal branding, ensuring that students present themselves genuinely.

Teachers and trainers, on the other hand, can integrate personal branding into the curriculum. They can create assignments and activities that promote self-awareness, teamwork and communication skills. By incorporating personal branding into the learning process, teachers can equip students with the necessary tools to thrive not only academically but also in their personal and professional lives.

The chapter also explores various techniques and resources that students can utilize to build their personal brand. From crafting an impactful resume and developing an online presence to networking effectively and building a professional image, students will gain practical insights into shaping their personal brand.

In conclusion, personal branding is an essential aspect of personality development for students. By understanding and cultivating their personal brand, students can unlock their true potential, stand out from the crowd and achieve their goals. This chapter aims to guide students, parents, teachers and trainers in recognizing the importance of personal branding for students and providing them with the necessary strategies and tools to embark on this transformative journey.

Building a Strong Online Presence

In today's digital age, having a strong online presence is crucial for students to succeed in their personal and professional lives. This chapter will explore the importance of building a strong online presence and provide practical tips and strategies for students to enhance their digital footprint.

The internet has become an integral part of our lives and students need to understand how their online presence can impact their reputation and future opportunities. Potential employers, college admissions officers and even peers often search for individuals online to gather information and form opinions. Therefore, students must curate a positive and professional online image.

First and foremost, students must be mindful of the content they share on social media platforms. Posting inappropriate or offensive material can have serious consequences and tarnish their reputation. It is crucial to think twice before sharing anything online and to consider the potential implications it may have.

Another important aspect of building a strong online presence is creating a professional online profile. Students should consider creating a LinkedIn account, which allows them to showcase their skills, achievements and interests to potential employers or college admissions officers. Maintaining an up-to-date resume and including relevant experiences and accomplishments can greatly enhance their online professional image.

Furthermore, students should actively engage with their online communities. This can be achieved by participating in online forums, joining relevant groups or contributing to discussions on platforms such as LinkedIn or industry-specific forums. By sharing thought-provoking insights and valuable information, students can establish themselves as knowledgeable and engaged individuals within their chosen fields.

Lastly, students should ensure that their online presence aligns with their personal brand and career goals. They should be consistent with their messaging and image across all online platforms. By demonstrating a clear and focused online presence, students can attract opportunities that are in line with their aspirations.

In conclusion, building a strong online presence is vital for students in today's digital world. By being mindful of their online activities, creating a professional profile, actively engaging with their communities and aligning their online presence with their personal brand, students can establish a positive and influential digital footprint. This chapter has provided students, parents, teachers and trainers with valuable insights and practical strategies to help students navigate and excel in building a strong online presence.

Developing Professional Skills and Networks

In today's digital world, it is essential for students to not only focus on academic excellence but also develop professional skills and networks. This section "Developing Professional Skills and Networks" from the book "Building Strong Foundations: Personality Development for Students" aims to guide students, parents, teachers and trainers on the importance of honing these skills and building a strong network for future success.

Professional skills encompass a wide range of abilities that go beyond academic knowledge. These skills include ***effective communication, teamwork, problem-solving, time management, leadership and adaptability***. The book emphasizes that developing these skills early on can significantly enhance a student's chances of success in their personal and professional lives. Practical advice and exercises are provided to help students identify their strengths and areas for improvement and strategies are outlined to develop these skills systematically.

Moreover, the chapter stresses the significance of building a strong professional network. A well-established network can offer valuable opportunities such as internships, mentorships, job referrals and collaborations. The book provides insights into how students can expand their networks through various means; including attending seminars, joining professional organizations, participating in extracurricular activities and leveraging social media platforms. It also offers guidance on how to maintain and nurture professional relationships to maximize their benefits in the long run.

The chapter also acknowledges the crucial role that parents, teachers and trainers play in helping students develop professional skills and networks. It offers practical tips for parents to support their children in identifying their career goals, encouraging them to participate in relevant activities and providing guidance on networking opportunities. Teachers and trainers are provided with strategies to incorporate professional skill development into their curriculums and create a supportive environment for students to practice and enhance these skills.

By focusing on developing professional skills and networks, students can gain a competitive edge in today's dynamic job market. This chapter aims to equip students, parents, teachers and trainers with the necessary tools and knowledge to navigate the process effectively. With a strong foundation in professional skills and networks, students can enhance their employability, foster personal growth and seize opportunities for success in their chosen fields.

Key Takeaways:

- Personal branding is about showcasing one's values, skills and passions.
- A professional approach helps students stand out in their career journey.

Call to Action Exercises:

For Students:

1. **Skills Assessment**: List your top skills and how you can use them to help others.
2. **Personal Brand Statement**: Create a one-sentence statement that highlights what makes you unique.
3. **Social Media Check**: Review your online profiles to ensure they reflect a positive image.

For Parents:

1. **Encourage Skill-Building**: Support your child in identifying and developing their strengths.

2. **Guide on Professionalism**: Talk about the importance of a good online reputation and behaviour.
3. **Set Professional Goals**: Help your child set one goal related to personal growth or skill improvement.

For Teachers/Trainers:

1. **Branding Workshop**: Teach students about personal branding and professional behaviour.
2. **Resume Building Activity**: Guide students to create a simple resume or list of achievements.
3. **Elevator Pitch Practice**: Have students practice introducing themselves with confidence.

Chapter 16
Celebrating Personal Growth and Success

Reflecting on Personal Growth and Achievements

As students embark on their journey of personality development, they must take the time to reflect on their personal growth and achievements. This chapter aims to guide students, parents, teachers and trainers in understanding the importance of reflection and its impact on the overall development of students.

Reflection is a powerful tool that enables individuals to gain self-awareness and make sense of their experiences. It allows students to look back on their journey, identify their strengths and weaknesses and set realistic goals for the future. Through reflection, students can assess their progress, celebrate their achievements and learn from their mistakes.

For students, reflection can lead to a deeper understanding of their personal values, interests and passions. By reflecting on their experiences, they can identify the activities that bring them joy and align with their aspirations. This self-awareness is invaluable as it helps students make informed decisions about their academic and career paths.

Parents play a crucial role in supporting their child's personal growth. By encouraging regular reflection, parents can help their children develop a growth mindset. They can create a safe and non-judgmental environment where their child can openly discuss their achievements, goals and challenges.

This open dialogue fosters a sense of trust and empowerment, allowing students to take ownership of their personal development.

Teachers and trainers also have a vital role in facilitating reflection among students. By incorporating reflective activities into their curriculum, they can help students process and internalize the knowledge they have gained. Through guided reflection, teachers can encourage students to connect their learning to real-life situations and develop critical thinking skills.

Ultimately, reflection is an ongoing process that should be integrated into the daily lives of students. It allows them to appreciate their progress, learn from their experiences and grow as individuals. By cultivating a habit of reflection, students can develop a strong sense of self and make informed choices that align with their personal values and goals.

In conclusion, this chapter emphasizes the significance of reflecting on personal growth and achievements for students. It highlights the role of parents, teachers and trainers in supporting and guiding students through this reflective process. By engaging in regular reflection, students can gain self-awareness, identify their passions and make informed decisions about their personal development.

Setting New Goals for Future Development

As we embark on our journey of personality development, it is essential to set new goals for our future development. Goals act as guiding stars, helping us stay focused, motivated and on track to achieve our dreams. In this chapter, we will explore the importance of setting new goals and how they can positively impact our personal growth.

For Students:

Setting new goals is crucial for students as they navigate through their academic journey. By identifying specific objectives, such as improving time management or enhancing study skills, students can enhance their academic performance. Additionally, setting goals related to personal growth, such as building self-confidence or improving communication skills, can help students excel in various aspects of their lives.

For Parents:

Parents play a vital role in guiding their children towards setting meaningful goals. By encouraging their children to set goals, parents can instill a sense of purpose and ambition. Parents can also help their children identify achievable goals and create action plans towards achieving them. This process helps develop essential life skills such as resilience, determination and perseverance.

For Teachers and Trainers:

Teachers and trainers have the responsibility to create an environment that fosters goal-setting and personal development. By incorporating goal-setting activities into the curriculum, educators can empower students to take charge of their growth. Providing guidance and support throughout the goal-setting process can help students develop essential skills, such as problem-solving, critical thinking and self-reflection.

Setting goals is not only about achieving tangible outcomes; it is also about personal growth and self-discovery. As we set new goals, it is important to remember that they should be SMART – Specific, Measurable, Achievable, Relevant and Time-bound. This framework ensures that goals are well-defined and attainable.

Furthermore, it is essential to regularly review and revise goals as circumstances and priorities change. By reflecting on our progress, we can identify areas for improvement and make necessary adjustments to our goals.

In conclusion, setting new goals for future development is a crucial step in the journey of personality development for students. By setting SMART goals, we can enhance our personal growth, academic performance and overall well-being. As students, parents, teachers and trainers, let us embrace the power of goal-setting and pave the way for a brighter and more successful future.

Maintaining a Life-long Commitment to Personality Development

In today's fast-paced world, where competition is severe and success is highly valued, students must understand the significance of maintaining a life-long commitment to personality development. Personality development goes beyond academics; it encompasses the holistic growth of an individual, including their emotional, social and intellectual well-being. This chapter aims to guide students, parents, teachers and trainers on how to nurture and sustain a life-long commitment to personality development.

First and foremost, students must understand that personality development is an ongoing process and that it requires continuous effort and self-reflection. It is essential to set clear goals and objectives for personal growth and self-improvement. By identifying areas of strengths and weaknesses, students can work towards enhancing their strengths while addressing their weaknesses effectively.

To maintain a life-long commitment to personality development, students must cultivate a growth mindset. They should embrace challenges, be open to learning from failures and seek opportunities for personal and professional growth. By adopting a growth mindset, students can develop resilience, perseverance and adaptability, which are essential qualities in today's dynamic world.

Parents play a pivotal role in nurturing a life-long commitment to personality development. They should encourage their children to explore their interests, pursue hobbies and engage in extracurricular activities that promote personal growth. Additionally, parents should foster a positive and supportive environment at home, where open communication and constructive feedback are encouraged.

Teachers and trainers also have a responsibility to facilitate personality development in students. They should create a classroom environment that encourages collaboration, critical thinking and creativity. By providing students with opportunities for self-expression, problem-solving and decision-making, teachers can empower them to take ownership of their personal growth.

Furthermore, students should actively seek out mentors and role models who inspire and motivate them. Mentors can provide valuable guidance, share their experiences and offer advice on navigating various challenges and opportunities. By forming meaningful connections with mentors, students can gain valuable insights and perspectives, which can significantly contribute to their personality development.

In conclusion, maintaining a life-long commitment to personality development is crucial for students. By setting clear goals, cultivating a growth mindset and seeking support from parents, teachers and mentors, students can develop into well-rounded individuals. Embracing personal growth and continuous self-improvement will not only enhance their academic performance but also equip them with the necessary skills to succeed in all aspects of life.

Key Takeaways:

- Celebrating achievements reinforces confidence and motivation.
- Reflection on growth helps students recognize how far they have come and where they can still go.

Call to Action Exercises:

For Students:

1. **Growth Journal**: Write down one area where you've improved over the past year.
2. **Personal Success Celebration**: Treat yourself to something small for each success.
3. **Reflect on Goals**: Look back at your goals and note which ones you've achieved.

For Parents:

1. **Celebrate Milestones**: Recognize and celebrate your child's progress in any area of growth.
2. **Reflect on Growth**: Have a conversation with your child about what they're proud of this year.

3. **Encourage New Goals**: Support your child in setting new goals to keep up the momentum.

For Teachers/Trainers:

1. **Progress Showcase**: Create an event or time for students to showcase their achievements.
2. **Achievement Reflection**: Encourage students to share their growth over the term.
3. **Goal-Setting Session**: Guide students in setting new personal or academic goals for the future.

Chapter 17 Conclusion - A Foundation for Life-long Success

As we come to the culmination of "Building Strong Foundations: Personality Development for Students," I am filled with a sense of fulfillment and optimism. This concluding chapter serves as a reflection on the transformative journey we've undertaken together and a guidepost for the exciting road ahead.

Throughout this book, we have explored the multifaceted dimensions of personality development, delving into the intricacies of self-awareness, goal setting, effective communication, emotional intelligence and numerous other vital aspects. Each chapter has been a stepping stone, carefully placed to construct a strong foundation upon which students can build a future of resilience, success and personal fulfillment.

Now, as we conclude our exploration, it is essential to recognize that the journey of personality development is not a destination but a life-long process. The skills and insights gained from these pages are not mere tools for the present but enduring companions for the future. It is my sincere hope that the knowledge imparted here will serve as a compass, guiding students through the complexities of life and aiding them in making informed decisions that align with their values and aspirations.

In this final chapter, let us reiterate some key takeaways:

1. Self-Discovery is Ongoing:

Personality development is a continuous process of self-discovery. Embrace change, learn from experiences and adapt as you evolve. Your journey of self-improvement is dynamic and uniquely yours.

2. Building Resilience:

Life is replete with challenges, but the ability to bounce back and learn from adversity is what defines true resilience. Equip yourself with the mental fortitude to navigate obstacles, emerging stronger on the other side.

3. Life-long Learning:

The pursuit of knowledge should be a life-long commitment. Stay curious, explore new horizons and engage in continuous learning. The world is vast and your capacity for growth is limitless.

4. Cultivating Empathy:

In a world that thrives on connection, empathy is a powerful force. Nurture your ability to understand and resonate with the experiences of others. By fostering empathy, you contribute to a more compassionate and inclusive world.

5. Personal Branding:

Your unique qualities and values shape your personal brand. Be intentional in crafting an authentic identity that reflects your strengths, aspirations and the positive impact you wish to make on the world.

6. Celebrating Success:

Acknowledge and celebrate your achievements, no matter how small. Cultivate a mindset of gratitude and use success as motivation for further growth.

7. Paying It Forward:

As you embark on your journey of personal development, consider how you can contribute to the growth and well-being of others. Whether through mentorship, support or acts of kindness, creating a positive ripple effect can be profoundly rewarding.

In conclusion, "Building Strong Foundations" is not a conclusion but a commencement—a starting point for a life rich in purpose, fulfillment and achievement. It is my avid wish that the principles and practices shared in these pages accompany you on your journey, providing guidance and inspiration for the remarkable journey that awaits.

As you step into the future, remember: the foundation is laid, the path is illuminated and the potential within you is boundless. May your journey be marked by continuous growth, unwavering resilience and the realization of your most ambitious dreams.

Wishing you a future filled with success, fulfillment and the joy of perpetual self-discovery.

Dr. Ravindran.K.A.

HR Management Professional, Transformation Coach & Author

Key Takeaways:

- Personality development is a continuous journey, impacting all areas of life.
- The foundations built now will support students in achieving future success and personal fulfillment.

Call to Action Exercises:

For Students:

1. **Future Vision Board**: Create a vision board with images and words representing your dreams.
2. **Identify Future Goals**: List three life goals you want to achieve and one step you can take now toward each.
3. **Ongoing Reflection**: Dedicate time each month to revisit and update your goals and progress.

For Parents:

1. **Discuss the Future**: Talk to your child about their dreams and how they plan to achieve them.
2. **Create a Family Vision Board**: Set family goals that support everyone's personal growth.

3. **Monthly Goal Check-In**: Have regular conversations about your child's evolving goals and progress.

For Teachers/Trainers:

1. **Personal Success Project**: Encourage students to create projects about their future dreams.
2. **Reflection Circle**: Discuss the importance of ongoing personal development with students.
3. **Goal Continuation**: Help students develop a plan to continue their growth beyond the classroom.

At the end let me say

Some of these strategies/successful practices you may have read or come across before.

But here's the deal: Your life won't change until your HABITS and PRACTICES change.

Merely reading or consuming success material doesn't change your life. I would encourage you to select your requisite strategy from this book and implement it in your daily life/organisation IMMEDIATELY.

Slowly but surely, you will begin to achieve things you never thought would have been possible...

If you liked this book, do consider leaving a review on Amazon. It only takes a few minutes but would help and motivate me to write more books.

I recommend you also read my other publications, titled

1. "Build a High-Performance Culture"

2. "High-Productivity Practices – From Successful Leaders – A Road to Success"

3. "What Great Managers Do Differently – Unlocking the Secrets of Extraordinary Leadership and Management"

4. 'Toxic Workplace: Identification, Prevention and Healing

These books are available on www.amazon.com or www.hroptimum.com

For other reading materials on HR management, please visit my blogging website https://hroptimum.com.

Your suggestions and feedback would be most welcome. You may kindly do so at: coach.drravindran@gmail.com

Thank you so much! Happy Reading! Keep Reading and grow steadily.

Acknowledgements

As I stand at the completion of "Building Strong Foundations: Personality Development for Students," I am filled with gratitude and appreciation for the collective effort and support that made this endeavour possible. Writing this book has been a journey of inspiration, growth and collaboration and I am indebted to many individuals and entities for their invaluable contributions.

First and foremost, I extend my deepest gratitude to the students whose stories, challenges and triumphs have been a wellspring of inspiration. Your enthusiasm for personal development and commitment to growth have fuelled the pages of this book. It is my sincere hope that the insights shared here resonate with you on your journey towards life-long success.

To the educators, mentors and counsellors who tirelessly guide and shape the minds of the next generation, thank you for your dedication. Your influence is immeasurable and your commitment to fostering personal development in students is commendable. This book is a tribute to the impactful work you do every day.

I extend my appreciation to my colleagues in the field of Human Resource management and personal development. Your shared experiences, diverse perspectives and collaborative spirit have enriched the content of this book. Together, we strive to positively impact the lives of individuals seeking personal growth and success.

A special acknowledgement goes to, whose expertise and insights have greatly contributed to the development of certain chapters in this book. Your guidance and collaboration have been instrumental in ensuring the depth and relevance of the content.

I am deeply grateful to my editor Mr. Saheesh Mohandas, whose keen eye and thoughtful feedback have greatly enhanced the clarity and coherence of this book. Your dedication and meticulous attention to detail have been invaluable.

I would like to express my gratitude to the publishing team at Guided Self Publishing (I) LLP, whose professionalism and support have been invaluable throughout the publication process. Your commitment to excellence has played a significant role in bringing this book to fruition.

To my family and friends, thank you for your unwavering support, encouragement and understanding during the writing process. Your belief in me has been a constant source of motivation and I am truly fortunate to have you in my corner.

Last but not least, to the readers who embark on this journey of self-discovery and personal development, I extend my heartfelt appreciation. Your engagement with the material is what gives it life and purpose. May this book serve as a guiding light on your path towards building strong foundations and unlocking the doors to your limitless potential.

In gratitude,

Dr. Ravindran. K.A.
HR Management Professional, Transformation Coach & Author

"What we think, we become"

– Buddha